THE BASIC BOOK OF
THE CAT

THE BASIC BOOK OF
THE CAT

BY WILLIAM H. A. CARR

GRAMERCY PUBLISHING COMPANY
New York

Printed in the United States of America

Library of Congress Catalog Card Number 62-20978

This edition published by Gramercy Publishing Company,
a division of Crown Publishers, Inc.,
by arrangement with Charles Scribner's Sons.

E F G H

TO **JEANETTE**

ACKNOWLEDGMENTS

Quotations from a number of other published works have been used in this book. For permission to use this material, and for other assistance, I wish to thank Mr. Raymond D. Smith, publisher of *Cats Magazine;* Mr. Frank E. Dittrich, publisher of *All-Pets Magazine* and of All-Pets Books, Inc.; Dr. Edwin H. Colbert of the American Museum of Natural History; Dr. Mark Morris and Mark Morris Associates, Inc.; Dr. S. N. Gershoff, of the Department of Nutrition, Harvard School of Public Health; the staff of the National Academy of Sciences-National Research Council; Mrs. Christine Stevens, president of the Animal Welfare Institute; the staff of the American Museum of Natural History; Mr. Howard Kaslow, of the U. S. Vitamin and Pharmaceutical Corporation; and Mr. Charles Melman, of Lifespan Products Company, Inc.

My fellow newspaperman, Mr. Henry Beckett, a felinophile of the first rank, has been very helpful.

I owe a special debt of gratitude to Fred J. Badger, D. V. M., whose constructive criticisms were invaluable.

Of course, only the author is responsible for the text.

PREFACE

CATS are like greatness—some people are born into cat-loving families, some achieve cats, and some have cats thrust upon them.

It is with a certain pride that I say that I achieved cats. Dogs were a part of my life from childhood, but cats I viewed with distrust and distaste until well into my adult years. Then I began to appreciate, very slowly at first, the admirable qualities of a friend's cat, Theodora. The friend, finding a sucker in his very living room, promptly presented me with one of Theo's kittens, a tabby whom I named Tammany (because he was tiger-striped and had the morals of that political institution). A few weeks later a big short-haired blue cat ventured through the window to investigate Tammany and to steal his food. In a day or two the blue had made himself quite at home. I had been adopted as his companion and provider. He was Mr. Gray.

Dogs are still a major part of my life, but I cannot conceive of a life without cats now. There is usually a clowder of cats (that's the proper noun of assembly for a group of cats—a *kendle* is a group of kittens) about me as I write. Nutcake sometimes insists on perching on top of my head. Pyewacket is happiest lying on my shoulders. Poor deaf Muffin is content to curl up and sleep in a nearby armchair. But Dulcie likes to sit on top of the typewriter; I'm sure she knows that when she's there I can't write, and so I'll pet her instead.

The affinity of writers for cats is something that has never been satisfactorily explained, to the best of my knowledge. Certainly a writer should have a special appreciation of esthetics, and few things in life are as esthetically pleasing as the graceful cat. But perhaps part of the reason for this attitude of writers lies in the skepticism which a writer ought to practice. A writer should be more inclined than other people to examine prejudices coolly. And the only thing that stands between most people and cats is prejudice (on the part of the people).

As every cat owner knows, cats are not sneaky. Their attempts at stealth during cat games are often hilarious failures. Cats are not treacherous. I've never heard of a cat turning on its owner (although some owners who insist on playing teasing games will get scratched). On the other hand, cats *are* affectionate, sometimes almost too affectionate. They are intelligent, clean, and endowed with a sense of humor that enables them to find human foibles endlessly diverting.

They deserve the kind of care that will enable them to live for many long, healthy years as companions to their human families. It is the purpose of this book to make it as easy as possible for the average cat owner to provide that kind of care for his cats.

CONTENTS

1. THE CAT FAMILY

"Wild beasts He created later,
Lions with their paws so furious;
In the image of the lion
Made He kittens small and curious."

—HEINRICH HEINE (1797-1856)
(translated by Edward A. Browning)

MYSTERY and the cat are synonymous. As Sir Walter Scott said to Washington Irving, "Ah! cats are a mysterious kind of folk." There are two million more cats than dogs in the United States, and yet we know very little about the cat, in contrast with our enormous store of knowledge about the dog.

Zoologists have many theories but few facts about the domestic cat and its wild cousins. We do not know when the cat was domesticated, or where. We do not know from what wild cats it was bred. We do not know whether it spread throughout the world from a single original site or whether it became a domestic animal at about the same time in several parts of the world. We do not know how many breeds of domestic cat exist in the world, and we do not know how many wild animals still prowling the earth belong to the cat family. To compound the confusion, zoologists disagree about the formal designation of the cat; one group argues that it is *felis domestica,* but a larger group insists that it must be referred to as *felis catus.*

Even our English word for a cat-hater, *ailurophobe,* is confusing; it was based on the belief that the mouse-killer mentioned in ancient

13

Greek writings was a cat, but we now know that it was some member of the weasel family, probably the marten or polecat.

To cap our ignorance, we do not even know the origin of the word *cat*. Little wonder that the tabby on the hearth has such an inscrutable expression!

Despite this unfortunate lack of proved facts about the cat, zoologists believe that they can make a great many educated guesses about the cat, its origins, and its relatives, and come quite close to the truth. These guesses are based on archeological findings, fossil remains, ancient paintings and writings, studies of mammalian evolutionary patterns, and our knowledge of the genetics of the present forms of the cat.

If the generally accepted theories are correct, the cat can be traced back to *Miacis*, a vicious, weasel-like little carnivore with a long body and short legs that existed on the earth about fifty million years ago. *Miacis* is also considered the ancestor of the dog, the hyena, the raccoon, the bear, the weasel, and the civet families. Apparently the cat descended from *Miacis* through the civet, a curious little animal which occurs in several forms today—one of them is the famous, snake-killing mongoose—in Africa, Asia, and southern Europe. (The true civet is important to women; the secretion from its anal glands is, strangely, the best fixative for the most expensive perfumes.) A typical civet is about three feet long with short legs, a long, bushy tail, and a small head. The Germans call it, appropriately, the "half-cat."

It is believed that the first cats were evolved about ten million years after *Miacis* made its appearance. This was probably ten or twenty million years before the dog, as we know it, evolved. The transition from *Miacis* to civet to cat was abrupt, as evolutionary processes go, despite the millions of years that passed. "The cats . . . suddenly appeared," in the words of Dr. Edwin H. Colbert of the American Museum of Natural History. "One might say that certain civets jumped into the role of the cats with all the evolutionary rapidity of a quick-change artist in a hard-pressed double part."

The cats initially divided into two groups: *Dinictis* and *Hoplophoneus*. The latter was notable for its exaggerated upper canine teeth which were so big that nature had to provide the cat with a flange on the lower jaw to shield those teeth when the mouth was closed. A species of *Hoplophoneus,* which we usually call the saber-toothed tiger (it wasn't truly a tiger at all, but it was a great cat), has been pleasantly designated *Smilodon* by the paleontologists. As large as a lion, the saber-tooth wasn't very fast, but it was a formidable enemy of the huge, slow-moving beasts that shook the earth with their passing in those prehistoric times. *Smilodon* was able to open its jaws very wide, and it could then strike down with its terrible canine teeth, throwing the strength of its powerful neck and the weight of its massive body into the blow. But the time came when the slow-moving beasts which were *Smilodon's* natural prey began to die out, and the saber-tooth itself was too clumsy to adapt itself to catching more agile animals. And so the saber-tooth, like its prey, became extinct.

Not so *Dinictis.* From it sprang our modern cats. Fast-moving, lithe, highly adaptable, intelligent, strong, equipped with teeth marvelously designed for stabbing and tearing, *Dinictis* and its descendants were so well suited to the rigors of competitive existence that they have remained virtually unchanged, with minor exceptions, to this day. Indeed, every genus found on earth today has been identified in fossils dating back to the Pliocene epoch in Eurasia, and so have several genera now extinct.

The classic description of the cat as it has emerged into modern times is that of Dr. Colbert:

"Of all land-living carnivores, the cats are among the most completely specialized for a life of killing and for eating meat. They are very muscular, alert, supple carnivores, fully equipped for springing upon and destroying animals as large or larger than themselves. They generally hunt by stealth and catch their prey with a long bound or a short rush of great speed. The limbs are heavy and strong, and the feet are provided with sharp, retractile claws that are used for catching and holding their victims. The neck is very heavy to take up the severe shocks imposed by the violent action of the head and the teeth. The teeth are highly specialized for just two functions—stabbing and cutting. The canine teeth are therefore long and strong, and the carnassials are large, perfected shearing blades; the other teeth are reduced or completely suppressed. The smaller cats are adept tree-climbers, but the larger cats spend most of their time upon the ground."

These are the cats as they developed before man walked upon the earth, before the great Pleistocene glaciers covered much of the globe. They have been with us ever since in their varied forms—the great cats, the lesser cats, the domesticated cat. It has been said that "God made the cat in order to give man the pleasure of petting the tiger," and certainly most felinophiles are fascinated by the tiger in domestic cats—and, conversely, by the kitten in tigers. So let us now take a look at the incomparable and magnificent animals that comprise the cat family, wild and domestic, as we know it today—animals that command our admiration for their grace, their dignity, and their awesome powers of reasoning.

The art, science, or—as it usually turns out to be—argument of classifying living creatures is called *taxonomy*. The biologists who practice this curious specialty seldom agree with one another on anything except the importance of pigeonholes. In classifying cats, they have followed many different systems. Some believe the cats belong to one genus, *Felis*. Others list as many as twenty-eight distinct genera.

All this may be confusing to the taxonomists, but it doesn't trouble the cats, nor should it perplex you. For the purposes of this book, we shall follow those taxonomists who divide the cat into three genera: *Panthera* (the great cats), *Acinonyx* (the cheetah, which is quite different from other cats), and *Felis* (all the rest, including the cat that is, I hope, purring in your lap at this moment).

Since prehistoric times, most of the felines have moved between the Old World and the New, and a number of them have reached the extreme southern tip of South America. Before man began carrying them with him, the cats were distributed in every part of the world except Australia and its satellite islands and Madagascar (now called Malagasay). There are creatures in Australia called "native cats" and "tiger cats," but they are not cats at all, but marsupials whose correct name is dasyure. They don't look like cats, and why they were ever called cats is something that only an Australian could tell you. But the Aussies need not feel embarrassed about this. All over the world, including our own country, people have a way of putting the label "cat" on many creatures that are not.

The "polecat," for example, is not a cat; it is the ferret, part of the weasel family (although in America the skunk is sometimes called a polecat, too). Then there is the "bashful cat" of tropical Asia, which is actually a tiny, odd-looking primate called the loris. The "black cat" to which our Northern woodsmen sometimes refer is properly identified as a large species of marten. The "phoby cat" which pops up in the speech of back-country folk in America is the skunk. The "miner's cat" or "ring-tailed cat" is correctly designated the cacomistle, a pretty, furry little member of the raccoon family who makes a pleasant pet and is guaranteed to keep the premises cleared of rats.

Because of its skill at hiding and stalking, its camouflage, and its nocturnal and arboreal habits, the cat, in most of its species, is difficult to find. Hence we really cannot be sure that this quick survey of the world's cats is by any means complete. There are probably species in abundance that are unknown to the scientific world.

The *Panthera* known to us are the lion, the tiger, the leopard, the snow leopard (which is not a different variety of the leopard, but a distinctly different species), the clouded leopard, and the jaguar.

Despite his traditional title of "King of the Beasts," the lion is, in most respects, less impressive than the tiger. Lions and tigers can and do interbreed; if a male lion and a female tiger mate, the result is called a *liger*, but if the sire is a tiger and the dam a lioness, the cub is a *tiglon*. Nothing, it seems, is simple in the cat world.

Without their skins—a predicament in which they seldom, fortunately, find themselves—lions look identical to tigers. Generally a lion is smaller than its striped cousin. It is also less to be feared, being a disgraceful but rather engaging coward. Many things frighten the lion—flapping laundry, small children, a skunk-like little animal called the zorille, and so on.

From many points of view the lion is an attractive beast. It kills only when it is hungry, and makes several meals off the carcass. When it isn't hungry, it wouldn't harm a living thing, except perhaps to guard its young or to defend itself against real or fancied danger. Men have stood within a few feet of lions who were feeding, without any menacing actions by the lions. When a lion isn't hungry, antelopes and other animals can and do graze near it, knowing that they are safe.

Sometimes a lion will just turn bad, and that's another matter. Usually these are lions that are unable because of age or infirmity to kill desirable game. But a man-eating lion is a formidable creature. The most famous man-eaters were a pair of lions that held up construction of the Uganda Railway in Africa, just before the turn of the century, by devouring twenty-eight Indian laborers in addition to scores of African natives.

A lion can break a man's back with one blow of its paw. In making a kill of its natural prey, the lion crouches low, then springs forward in a dash that has been clocked at forty miles an hour.

Of all the cats, with the possible exception of the domestic cat, only the lion is gregarious. The usual pride of lions consists of five or six males and females; the latter usually kill the game which the males have driven in their direction.

"The known history of the lion," says Dr. Philip J. Darlington, Jr., of Harvard University's Museum of Comparative Zoology, "is . . . one of retreat before man during a period of nearly two thousand years." Within the period of recorded history, lions were to be found in southeast Europe as far north as Rumania and as far west as Italy, throughout all of Africa (except in the West African forests and the interior of the deserts), and in southwestern Asia as far as India's western provinces. The lion has been slowly withdrawing toward the heartland of Africa in modern times. There may be a few lingering survivors in Iraq and Iran, but the only known concentration outside Africa is in the Forest of Gir, Kathiawar, northwestern India, where they are protected. Even in Africa they have been on the retreat. There haven't been any lions in Cape Province, South Africa, for a century. In Algeria and Tunis the lion was last seen in 1891, although it managed to survive until the 1920's in neighboring Morocco. Now it is found in abundance only below the Sahara.

The lion is sometimes shown with the tiger in fanciful movie scenes, but in truth the two seldom if ever get together in the same locale in nature. There are no tigers in Africa and few lions, as has been noted, anywhere else.

The tiger is one of the most fascinating of the big cats, if only for its sometimes surprising habitats. It ranges from the far below zero cold of eastern Siberia to the intense heat of the jungles of southern India. The original home of the tiger was in or near the Arctic, zoologists generally believe, and the great Amurian tiger, sometimes called the Siberian snow tiger, is still the biggest of all the cats, attaining a total length of more than thirteen feet and a maximum weight in excess of six hundred and fifty pounds. Tigers gradually moved down through east and southeast Asia to India and the islands of Sumatra, Bali, and Java (but not, for some strange reason, Ceylon), and also, in a similar southwestward migration, from Siberia by way of central Asia to Afghanistan, Iran, and southern Russia all the way west to the Caucasus.

But the tiger has never forgotten the climate of its origin; in the well-nigh unbearable heat of the Malayan jungle, the tiger will go for a swim in the water to keep cool. Indeed, it loves to swim, as many of the cats do, although it hates to get just a little wet, as from the dew.

Tigers are universally feared as indiscriminate man-eaters, but we have the word of the ultimate expert on that subject, Jim Corbett, that this is a canard. Like the lion, the tiger makes man its prey only when it is unable to obtain its preferred natural food. A tiger, unless molested, will do no harm to man, says Lieutenant Colonel Corbett in his fascinating book, *Man-Eaters of Kumaon,* a recounting of his true experiences as India's foremost exterminator of man-eating tigers and leopards. "I have not seen a case where a tiger has been deliberately cruel or where it has been bloodthirsty to the extent that it has killed, without provocation, more than it has needed to satisfy its hunger or the hunger of its cubs," writes Corbett. And there has been no better salute to an honored foe than his statement on the tiger's character: "A tiger is a large-hearted gentleman with boundless courage."

There is a considerable variation in the ground color of the tiger, ranging all the way from the most common bright reddish-orange to eggshell white. The only black-and-white tiger in captivity outside

India is Enchantress, a blue-eyed beauty in the Smithsonian Institution's National Zoological Park at Washington, D.C., which was obtained from Rewa, one of the few regions of India where white tigers abound.

The white tigers probably reflect an albino strain in the species. Just the opposite is true of the leopards: albinos are unknown, but a tendency toward melanism—that is, black mutation—is marked. The black leopard is usually referred to popularly as a black "panther," although properly the panther is any great cat that can roar.

Leopards are far deadlier than lions or tigers; they can become man-eaters simply because they acquire a taste for human flesh. Somewhat hysterical and easily frightened, they are night hunters and anything living is their prey, including farm animals, fowl, dogs, and monkeys. Somewhat smaller than the lion and the tiger, the leopard is really more dangerous, for it often takes to the trees, adding a new dimension to the menace of the big cats. It is also incredibly intelligent; sometimes a leopard will roll crazily on the ground to excite curiosity in a herd of antelope and lure them close enough to be killed.

The British Isles were once home to the leopard. Its range extended all the way east to Japan and south throughout all of Asia except for the Himalayan highlands. It was also found on Ceylon and the Indonesian islands. Today it is still found in the Caucasus—which remains a sort of unintentional refuge for many harried forms of fauna—and even in Siberia, as well as throughout east and southeast Asia, the Middle East, and all of Africa.

The snow leopard is also called the *ounce*, a word that comes through Old French and Middle English from the Latin *lynx*, strangely enough. It lives in the thin-aired upper reaches of the Asian mountains from the Himalayas north to Siberia and Sakhalin Island. Its double coat protects it against the intense cold it must endure, and its colors —whitish gray with yellow rings on the back and plain white on the belly—are not as flamboyant as those of its jungle cousins, and thus not as easily noticed by its prey on the mountainous heights.

The clouded leopard is one of the smallest, rarest, and most beautiful of cats. Its body is only about three feet long, although it has a tail disproportionately long for its body. Its thick, full, soft fur is gray or grayish-yellow, marked with small, square-shaped black forms with dark brown in the center. There are stripes on the face, spots on the legs, and rings on the tail. It has the longest canine teeth of any cat. A nocturnal prowler that sleeps in the day, it can seldom be detected in its natural habitat, which ranges from South China to Sumatra and Borneo, in addition to the island of Formosa.

The only American cat among the *Panthera* is the jaguar, inaccurately but commonly called "el tigre" by our Latin-American neighbors. Its range in the past was from the mountains of the southeast United States (principally Arizona and New Mexico) south to the Santa Cruz River in Patagonia, near the southern tip of South America. But some authorities believe that the jaguar now can be found only in the Chaco, a vast region in northern Argentina, Bolivia, and Paraguay. This may be incorrect, however. Jaguars have reportedly been sighted in 1956 near Ruby, Arizona, northwest of Nogales, in 1958 in the Patagonia Mountains east of Nogales, and in 1960 in the Sonora River Valley close to the Arizona-Mexico border.

This spotted cat, the best tree-climber of all the great cats, likes both humid jungle and arid desert. It may occur as an albino or as a black mutation. It enjoys swimming so much that it will pursue its prey into the water and will even tackle an alligator in a stream. It is renowned for its ferocity, but some zoologists assert that not a single human killing by a jaguar has been authenticated.

In the genus *Acinonyx* there is only one species, the cheetah, although it is possible that this may be found in two or three varieties sufficiently distinct to be called species. The cheetah is the famous hunting cat. The most tractable large cat, it makes an excellent pet and can be trained easily. Since ancient times cheetahs have been domesticated in Egypt and in India and other Asian lands as hunters and retrievers. These amazingly fleet creatures—they have been clocked at sixty miles per hour and it's believed they sometimes reach seventy-five—are rather like coursing hounds. They are kept, not in a cage, but simply on a chain. On a hunt they are hooded until the quarry is sighted; then the hood is removed and the cheetah dashes after the prey, knocks it down, and holds it by the throat. They have been used to kill coyotes in the United States.

Like the dog, the cheetah's claws are only partly retractile.

Once widespread in Africa and southwestern Asia, the cheetah is now so close to extinction that a conservation program aimed at saving these unique and wonderful animals has been established.

Genus *Felis* includes a number of unusual cats in addition to our domestic cat: the puma, the golden cats, the jaguarundi, the ocelot, the margay, the serval, the lynx, the bobcat.

The puma—or cougar, or mountain lion, as it is also called—is the second largest American cat (after the jaguar). It is also one of the most misunderstood and maligned. These cats are often accused by ranchers in the United States of the wanton slaughter of domestic livestock. Although the puma will sometimes kill a calf, its usual prey is small mammals which are themselves serious pests, and so it is really helpful in maintaining the balance of nature and keeping down the farmer's worst enemies. It is one of the most timid of cats; there are scarcely any reliable accounts of a puma's having attacked a man. In short, there is no reason for hunting the puma, except for the occasional cat that may become a persistent marauder.

The body of the puma is long and lithe; it carries about 160 pounds of weight on its six-foot frame, and amazing strength is built into it, for a puma can drag five times its own weight more than a hundred yards. It is rather oddly put together, with its hindquarters higher and more prominent than its head and chest, probably because it spends so much of its time leaping into trees and onto crags. It can spring twenty feet in one jump.

The nonsense that is retailed about the puma and its "savagery" is appalling. I have personally enjoyed petting a puma and gently tickling it under the chin, and the big cat acted like a kitten. Several members of the Long Island Ocelot Club, which takes in all the exotic cats, keep pumas as pets. Two members of the club, Ray and Daphne Ovington, recently reported in the club's newsletter on an incident that must have enlivened things in Woodstock, New York. "We were staying at a motel before we 'closed' on our house," wrote Mrs. Ovington. "Ray was taking some boxes out to the car. Quick as a flash, before the screen door closed, Winnie [the cougar] dashed from across the room out the door, ran behind the motel, up the hill which was heavily wooded. She hid there. The forest ranger brought two of his best bobcat and coon dogs and tried to get her trail but of no avail. She had her collar on and we were afraid it would choke her with growth as it was already getting snug. She was afraid of people. Her instinct told her to lie low in the leaves or to run when approached. She was seen on someone's back porch several times. People were seeing her every day from their cars crossing a road or walking around a corner of a house, but by the time they called us and we arrived, she was nowhere to be found. Finally we set a box trap with meat. After eleven days of being out we found her sitting in the trap one evening. We brought her, trap and all, wild and frightened, to the house. She was very hungry and 'beat' and she had grown quite a bit. We were worried about her disposition, but the next day she was nuzzling me and purring and seemed to be very happy to be home again. She is even more gentle and affectionate now than she was before."

The puma had one of the farthest ranges of any animal—from the Arctic to the Straits of Magellan, throughout the entire Western Hemisphere. Today it is generally believed by zoologists that it is limited to the Canadian Rockies, the mountains in the western states, and throughout most of Central and South America. There are also probably a few left in Florida and Louisiana.

But that's not all. The puma may be closer to some of our urban centers than we assume. In 1958 William V. Garner, professor of biology at Monmouth College, who has observed mountain lions in their natural surroundings, was startled to see a cougar on the shoulder of the Garden State Parkway near Long Branch, New Jersey, less than thirty miles from New York City. A businessman of New York, Ludwig K. Moorehead, collects reports of puma sightings in his area. He has more than forty reports in his file of cougars spotted in New York, New Jersey, Vermont, New Hampshire, and Massachusetts. There have also been well authenticated sightings in Virginia, the Carolinas, Alabama, Missouri, and Minnesota in recent years.

If pumas are about us, even in small numbers, one might expect to see them more often. But this would be wrong. D. D. McLean of the California Fish and Game Department, who regards the cougar as "our least known large mammal," has pointed out that "people living in lion country may go through an entire lifetime without as much as a fleeting glimpse of one of the big cats."

The golden cats are not found in America. They are two rather similar species of felines, one of which is found in Asia, the other in central and west Africa, both about the size of a leopard—indeed, the Chinese call their golden cat *huang pao,* meaning "yellow leopard". There could be another reason besides their color for the name of these cats, for both species are an item of trade: the Chinese sell the bones of *huang pao* in their medicine shops and some African natives chop the whiskers of their golden cats to make a poison said to be fatal to humans. (Whether it is fatal, and if so, why, I really don't know.)

The serval proves, beyond dispute, that cats, individualists as they are, will not permit themselves to be lumped indiscriminately together by taxonomists. This is a short-tailed cat with the long legs of a greyhound, and with good reason, for the serval lives on the open plains of equatorial Africa and runs down its quarry, usually small animals, birds, and lizards. Ignore its hide and its distinctly catty head, and the serval looks very much like a dog.

The jaguarundi is any of several varieties of closely related cats that can be found anywhere from the southwestern United States to southern Chile west of the Andes. They are also called the eyra, the colocollo, and (in Mexico) the otter cat. None of the jaguarundis looks very much like a cat—with their long bodies and tails, short legs, and small heads, they really appear more weasel-like than feline. As you might expect, they have caused another argument among zoologists, some of whom think they shouldn't be classified with the cats at all.

Indeed, there is very little agreement among the experts on this genus of cat. One eminent zoologist says the jaguarundi is "a ferocious, untamable creature," while another equally respected zoologist says the jaguarundi was domesticated by the Indians of Paraguay before the discovery of America. The latter would appear to be right, for many jaguarundis now are being sold as pets by importers of exotic cats, and their owners appear to be happy with them.

The lynx is another strange-looking cat. Its hind legs are much longer than its forelegs, which gives it a peculiar posture, and its appearance is made still more remarkable by its stub of a tail, broad paws, extravagantly tufted ears, and profuse side-whiskers that look like the mutton-chop whiskers once favored by portly gentlemen. The lynx is found deep in the most remote forests of northern Europe and Asia. It is found in North America, too, but rarely below the Canadian border, although a few have been sighted in Colorado and Oregon. The large pads on the lynx's feet enable it to run swiftly over snow after its favorite prey, the snow rabbit.

Like the other cats, the lynx is famous for its intelligence. The Czech writer Stanek, speaking of the lynx, asserts that in the Tatra Mountains of Slovakia he found the footprints of a lynx carefully placed inside the footprints of a bear for more than a hundred yards. This is a favorite device of the lynx for baffling pursuers.

The bobcat is a variety of lynx that has a special attraction for Americans. It is a peculiarly American animal, being found throughout the United States, in southern Canada, and in northern Mexico. The Catskill Mountains of New York State were named for the bobcat by the explorer Henry Hudson (*Kaatskill* means Wildcat Creek). It is sometimes called a "catamount"—so is the puma, which makes for confusion—probably from the Spanish *gato monte* (woods cat). A more common label for it in the vernacular is "wild cat."

The bobcat is a pretty cat in its markings and its skull formation. It can be formidable, however: bobcats ranging in weight up to sixty-nine pounds and in length up to fifty-three inches have been killed by hunters.

"This Cat," wrote historian John Lawson back in 1718, "is quite different from those in Europe; being more nimble and fierce, and larger; his Tail does not exceed four inches. He makes a very odd sort of Cry in the Woods, in the Night. He is spotted as the Leopard is, tho some of them are not (which may happen, when their Furs are out of Season). He climbs a Tree very dexterously, and preys as the Panther does. . . . He takes most of his Prey by Surprize, getting up the Trees which they pass by or under, and thence leaping directly upon them. Thus he takes Deer (which he cannot catch by running) and fastens his Teeth into their Shoulders and sucks them. They run with him, till they fall down for want of strength, and become a Prey to the Enemy. Hares, Birds, and all he meets, that he can conquer, he destroys. . . . [His furs] are . . . used to line Muffs, and Coats withal, in cold Climates."

Bobcats, if taken young and reared in captivity, make excellent pets. Even when they are living in their natural wild state, bobcats often mate with domestic cats, and the offspring, too, are as engaging household company as any tabby.

N. P. Kenoyer, writing in *Cats Magazine,* described such a mating: "It was early evening when we heard the unmistakable howl of Tabbette, our dark, striped cat. We rushed outside to see what neighbor's tomcat was courting our pet. We stopped short when we saw the two animals. It was not a neighbor's tom. The two cats faced each other, snarling and howling. Tabbette hugged the ground, her ears laid back tight against her head and her lips pressed against her teeth. This attitude was not unusual for her during this period, but her new, determined, prospective mate was. He was a young bobcat, long-legged, slim-bodied, with a mixture of strips and spots running down his legs."

The account then reported on the results of the crossbreeding. "Two months later Tabbette had five dark, tabby, stubby-tailed kittens," the writer said. "Some were tinged with reddish fur running along the soft undersides of their bellies. The tails were of different lengths but all bobbed. Their hind legs were unusually long and powerful and it became more apparent when they were old enough to run about. They hopped like rabbits except when they ran. There were tiny tufts of hair at each ear tip. They froze in cautious stance when startled. But they were deeply affectionate and wanted to spend all their time with us. They acted more like dogs than cats. They didn't even meow like a domestic cat. Their purr was heavy and deep-toned and they growled as they played. They began to hunt even before they lost their kitten roundness. We had no trouble finding homes for these little half-breeds. We kept a male kitten which we named Stubby.

"Stubby grew fast. By the time he was a year old he stood fourteen inches high and weighed ten pounds. He had a daily routine which he followed like a time clock. He was early for breakfast, eating little but always consuming a full saucer of milk. He loved cookies and crackers and would leave meat if he heard the sound of the cookie jar lid. He was fond of our boxer dogs and they liked him. If the dogs napped he always found them and curled up close to their warm bodies. He would sleep all day but he wanted out at night. He ranged between our barn and that of our neighbor's. He kept both places free of mice.

"Stubby dispatched every tomcat who came within his boundaries. Our neighbor put out food for him but couldn't come within twenty feet without Stubby's racing away in the direction of home. Yet he liked people, if they were in our house. Visitors could expect to find him on their laps as soon as they sat down. But away from the house he would scream if cornered and his appearance was wild. However, the boys could pick him up anywhere. He chose our neighbor's Persian cat for a mate and soon there was a litter of short-tailed kittens. Stubby influenced the kittens with his conformation and disposition. Everyone who saw Stubby wanted one of his kittens. Now we are looking for a pure bobcat female for Stubby because, given a choice, we'd take a bobcat every time."

Another member of the lynx family is the caracal, a slender, long-eared, reddish-brown cat found in the drier areas of Africa, the Middle East, and India. (This cat should not be confused with the caracul, a sheep of central Asia which is known to most American women because its wool is often made into fur coats.) Except for the cheetah, the caracal is the most aberrant of the cats. Its ears are tufted, like those of its lynx cousins, but it lacks the distinctive lynx sideburns. The tail is about nine inches long, a rather short appendage to a body about two and a half feet long.

In India this handsome cat has often been kept as a pet in wealthy households; it takes training well. A fast runner and remarkable jumper, the caracal is able to run down gazelles and even to catch birds on the wing by leaping six feet or more into the air to strike them.

There is one other cat in the lynx branch of the cat family: the jungle cat, also called the African wild cat. This cat, which probably is one of the progenitors of our domestic cat, is a remarkable example of how misleading feline nomenclature can be. This "African" wild cat is found mostly outside Africa. It is, to be sure, a native of the eastern part of North Africa, but it is also widely distributed from India, Ceylon, Burma, and Yunnan China west to the Caucasus, including the entire Middle East. And it is *never* found in the jungles, as we customarily use that word, in the sense of a lush, humid, dense tropical forest. This cat is called the jungle cat because it prefers relatively open, hot, dry scrublands—and that's what the word *jangal*, from which "jungle" is derived, means in Hindustani.

This cat, described scientifically as *Felis chaus,* is found in several varieties, all of which are smaller than the other lynxes but larger than any of the other lesser cats. The largest form of the jungle cat is about thirty inches long and weighs up to twenty pounds. It has a rather wistful, haunting expression on its face, but this should not be permitted to encourage close approach by humans, for in captivity the jungle cat—or so some zoologists insist—remains shy of humans and untamed. (This is said incorrectly of so many other species of cat that one is inclined to doubt the accuracy of the statement when applied to the African wild cat, too.)

The African wild cat interbreeds freely with the domestic cat. Indeed, there is reason to believe that all of the smaller cats with which we are now concerned have mated at various times with the domesticated animal.

This is not to be wondered at, for these are the cats from which our domestic cat probably is sprung. There are a number of cats that are believed to have had a part in the development of the household feline. The major wild cats in its lineage are assumed to be the Kaffir cat (*Felis lybica*), a related wild cat (*Felis ocreata*), both natives of Africa, and the European wild cat (*Felis silvestris*), which survives today in remote parts of Scotland and in the forests of central and eastern Europe all the way to Asia. All three of these cats are marked like tabbies.

There are many other small wild cats in various parts of the world. Precisely how many different kinds of small wild cats there are we don't know; often it is questionable whether a cat that has been captured or killed is a different species, a mutation, or simply a different color of a known species. These small cats include the tiny Sebala cat of the Kalahari Desert in Africa and several other desert cats, among them the long-haired manul (Pallas' cat) of central Asia, the sand cat of southern Russia, and the desert cat of Iran. Argentina boasts a long-haired, tabby-marked grass cat in the pampas. In southeast Asia there are two monochromatic little cats, the bay cat of Borneo and the flat-headed cat. The small fishing civet of Malaya behaves like a member of the civet family.

The ocelot and the margay are the most familiar of the small wild cats. Both are American cats. Their range is from the southwestern states of our country to southern South America. They are marked somewhat like leopards. The margay is about the size of a house cat. The ocelot ranges in size from twenty to sixty pounds (which may indicate that what we believe to be a species is actually several species). The adaptability and tractability of the ocelot and the margay make these cats highly suitable as pets, with certain reservations (see Chapter 11).

Our own domestic cat (*Felis catus*) has been living with man for at least five thousand years. This may seem like a long time, but it is brief in comparison with the domestication of the dog, which probably occurred more than fifty thousand years ago. The cat may have been tamed first in the Nile Valley or simultaneously in various parts of the world; we really don't know. All that we do know for sure is that our oldest records of domesticated cats were found in Egyptian ruins. And we know that the house cat of the ancient Egyptians was somewhat like today's Abyssinian breed.

It was not until the fourth century A.D., or possibly a little earlier, that the word "cat" came into use. The origin of the word is, like almost everything else about the cat, shrouded in mystery—and yet it is an almost universal word. In literature the word first appears in the works of Palladius, who urges the use of the cat to protect artichoke gardens from rodents and moles; he calls the mouser *catus* (it was also written with two *t*'s in those days), and it is obvious that he didn't coin the word, but merely used a term already in popular use.

Today the word exists in recognizable form in many languages, including some which have no relationship to each other. Thus, the word is *kitt* in Arabic, *kadis* in Nubian, *kat* in Dutch, *katt* in Swedish, *gatto* in Italian, *gato* in Spanish and Portuguese, *kot* in Polish, *kots* in Russian, *keti* in Turkish, *cath* in Welsh, *kath* in Cornish, *chat* in French, *Katze* in German, *catua* in Basque, *kitta* in Armenian, and so on.

Linnaeus felt at home using *Felis catus* for the genus in 1758. Unfortunately, nobody seems to have noticed his designation of the domestic cat by that name, for in 1777 Erxleben called it *Felis domestica,* and so did Gmelin in 1788 and Fischer in 1829. By that time everybody was calling the wee beast *Felis domestica,* in public at least—and then came the belated discovery by some taxonomical busybody that Linnaeus had been the first to slap a label on the creature, and that the label was *Felis catus.* Under taxonomical rules, the first name applied is the permanent, official name. So all the scientists had to discard the use of *Felis domestica* in favor of *Felis catus.*

But it wasn't that easy. The term *Felis catus* was already in use for another member of the genus, the European wild cat. If the domestic cat was to become *Felis catus,* obviously a new name had to be found for the wild cat. So it became *Felis silvestris,* a name first bestowed upon it by Schreber in 1777. And thus this game of musical chairs appeared to have come to an end.

Not so. In recent years a movement has sprung up to change the names again. Some zoologists suggested that the whole process be revised, with the wild cat becoming *Felis catus* again, the domestic cat becoming *Felis domestica,* and the label *Felis silvestris* going into mothballs. Other zoologists suggested that the term *Felis catus* be extended to cover the wild cat as well as the domestic cat. But most of the zoologists, with the support of the more important cat fanciers, who were in danger of becoming thoroughly confused, decided that this sort of thing had gone on altogether too long. They decided that *Felis domestica* should not be resurrected and that the domestic cat should continue to be *Felis catus.*

And there the matter rests—at least for the present.

2. THE BREEDS

> "Cats are of divers colors; but for the most part gryseld like to congealed yse, which commeth from the condition of her meate; her head is like unto the head of a Lyon, except in her sharpe eares: her flesh is soft and smooth: her eies glister above measure especially when a man commeth to see a cat on the sudden, and in the night they can hardly be endured for their flaming aspect.
>
> "It is a neat and cleanely creature. . . ."
>
> —EDWARD TOPSELL, in *The Historie of Four-Footed Beastes* (1607)

As IT SPREAD throughout the world, the domestic cat mated readily with a great many of its small cousins. The result was a species of almost unbelievable variety in color, size, and structure. In some parts of the world certain strains struck the fancy of some cat owners. To perpetuate such a strain, the owner would segregate those cats so they could not breed with others. Inbreeding accentuated the special qualities of the strain, and soon each generation bred true. The strain was now a breed.

Most of our domestic cats, of course, belong to no particular breed, but to that great commonwealth of catdom which knows no law but the sovereignty of the individual. This same splendid independence is true also of those cats which can be classified within a breed, for nothing man has done has succeeded in changing the essential qualities of the cat—the intangible virtues that make it the embodiment of freedom.

If the presumptions about the origin of the domestic cat are correct, the type we usually call "tabby" is the closest to the earliest domesticated cats of Egypt and western Europe. There are two forms of tabby, the blotched and the striped. R. I. Pocock (1863-1947), who was probably the foremost expert on cats in the world, regarded the blotched variety (technically described as the *catus* pattern) as a mutation that "arose abruptly and fully developed" from the striped (or *torquata*) pattern.

The striped tabby has narrow stripes transversely or vertically arranged on the sides of the body behind the shoulders. Toward the posterior these markings have a tendency to break into shorter stripes or spots. There are ill-defined blackish markings toward the base of the tail. The blotched tabby, on the other hand, has broad stripes which usually are looped or spiraled behind the shoulders. There are generally three stripes on the back running to the root of the tail. "The two pattern-phrases . . . are individually variable to a certain extent," says Pocock, "but one or the other can be detected in a majority of skins at all events of European domestic cats, although the stripes on the body may be entirely suppressed in the *torquata*-phase, which is less stable than the *catus*-phase."

But the tabby is only the basic cat. Throughout the world, cross-breeding with wild cats, adaptation of color and coat to environment, and the spontaneous development of mutants brought into being a myriad of different kinds of cats—short-haired, long-haired—of almost every imaginable color.

Pocock lists some of the varieties: a tortoiseshell phase "supposed to have come from Spain," a blue-gray phase from Europe and Siberia, a red phase from the Cape of Good Hope, a black and yellow phase with pendulous ears from China, a reddish-yellow type with a long head and sharp snout from New Spain, a variety with a twisted tail "doubtless imported from Malaya, where the malformation is not uncommon," a blackish phase from South Africa, a gray-colored animal from Abyssinia, a black-and-white pattern from Japan, a piebald from the same country, a stunted-tailed cat of black and white, also from Japan, a fawn-and-black type from Thailand, and a black cat from southern Russia.

The world is full of many kinds of cats with which we are completely unfamiliar in this country. One such breed is the korat, a cat from Thailand. An article by Jean L. Johnson in *Cats Magazine* ex-

ABOVE: A litter of tabby short-hair kittens. Tabby markings are common to most cats, although they may be concealed by overlying coats.

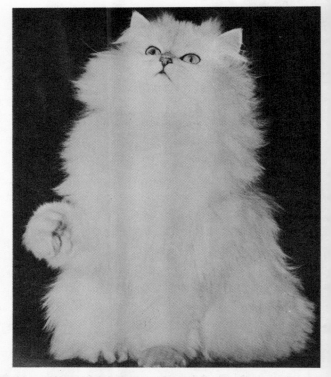

RIGHT: A cream long-hair kitten: *Bellham's Bonnie Heather,* owned by Mr. and Mrs. William A. Bellham.

ABOVE: This smoke long-hair and margay, *Sinbad* and *Monte* (for *Montezuma*), both owned by Mrs. Meg Merrill, are devoted friends.

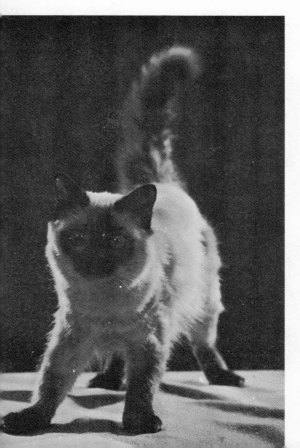

LEFT: A long-hair seal-point mutation bred from pure-bred Siamese stock. By careful inbreeding, the owner, Mrs. Helen Smith, has been able to produce sixteen additional blue and chocolate-point long-hair Siamese. These are true mutations, tracing their pedigrees back through many generations of short-hair Siamese. For a comparison with a Himalayan, turn two pages.

PHOTO: KENNETH R. SANDERSON, INC.

RIGHT: A lilac-point Siamese, *Si-cat's Sheermist of Gables,* a quadruple champion queen owned by Sam and Lily Scheer, has been one of the top winning Siamese.

BELOW: An Abyssinian: *Selene's Garnette,* a triple champion owned by Mr. and Mrs. Leonard Schuler. The horizontal dark markings near the nose and the ticking on the body are typical of Abyssinians.

PHOTO BY "MUZZIE"

ABOVE: A Russian Blue: *Sherwood Natasha*, bred and owned by Mrs. Florence Kanoffe.   PHOTO: LOUIS LIOTTA

BELOW: A tortoiseshell short-hair: *Cardell's Indian Summer*, owned by Mrs. Vera M. Cronin.   PHOTO: LOUIS LIOTTA

ABOVE: A red tabby Manx: *Guthred of Manx of Glen Orry,* a grand champion bred and owned by the Misses Ruth and Ellen Carlson.

BELOW: A tortoiseshell long-hair: *Elco's Starella of Cheri-Sue,* owned by Mrs. Vera M. Cronin.   PHOTO: LOUIS LIOTTA

ABOVE: A black short-hair: *Silhouette of Sal-Dan,* owned by Mrs. Donald O. Burow.

LEFT, TOP: *Muffin,* a white domestic short-hair, owned by the author.

MIDDLE: A Himalayan kitten, *Homestead's Sinbadi of Jamal,* at five months, owned by Mrs. T. J. Glad.

BELOW: A silver tabby short-hair: *Pussy Willow's Brutus III,* bred and owned by Mrs. Helen Newman.

BELOW: *Nutcake,* a Siamese-Burmese cross owned by the author. The coloring is typical of the Burmese, but the faint tabby bars on the hind legs would be a serious flaw in either breed.

RIGHT: Clipping the cat's nails: *Pyewacket* is restrained by its owner's arm and its claws are forced out by gentle pressure on its paws.

RIGHT: Brushing the cat: *Dulcie* is firmly restrained while her coat is brushed with long, steady strokes.

BELOW: One type of harness, with leash attached. Even an agile cat can't squirm out of this harness.

ABOVE: The essentials: a bag litter, a plastic or porcelain pan hold it, and a sieve to sift out t solid wastes daily.

plained how she and her husband had acquired a pair of korats. When they went to Bangkok after World War II, they decided that this sojourn in the homeland of the Siamese cat provided an excellent opportunity to get a cat of that breed. "We turned first to our new Siamese friends," Mrs. Johnson recalled. "Strangely, they did not seem to know anything about the cat as we described it!"

They did, however, tell her about a Siamese cat that was solid gray. They said this cat could only be found on the Korat Plateau, a wild and virtually unpopulated plain far from the capital—and even there she probably wouldn't be able to buy one because the natives prized them too much. These korat cats, solid gray with amber-green eyes, were rare and were "given only to the highest officials as a token of high esteem and affection," she learned. In six years of residence in Thailand she was unable to obtain such a cat.

In 1959, after the Johnsons had left Thailand and returned to the United States, a Siamese friend managed to obtain a male and a female korat for Mrs. Johnson. The korats were bred successfully and some of these cats now can be seen at a few cat shows. Mrs. Johnson hopes to establish the korat in time as a recognized breed here.

Another foreign breed recently introduced into America is the Tibetan temple cat, a long-haired colorpoint that looks, at first glance, rather like one of the breeds recognized here, the Himalayan. The Tibetan cats are a golden cream with body shading from cream to chocolate. The points are black, the eyes are blue. Mrs. R. C. Griswold plans to breed these cats in the United States.

We know that there have been curly-tailed cats in China (whether these were a distinct breed or simply occasional mutants is not clear, however), and that Africa has the Mombas cat, which has very short, stiff hair with a few long hairs as eyebrows, but with no eyelashes.

Ask any New England hunter and he'll tell you all about how the Maine coon cats result from the crossbreeding of cats with racoons. It's a fanciful idea, but it's totally false. Racoons belong to a completely different division of animals (they're closer to dogs than to cats, but they can't mate with dogs), and such a crossbreeding is, literally as well as figuratively, inconceivable. The so-called Maine coon cat is believed to be descended from long-haired tabbies that went feral (wild) centuries ago, after the early settlers brought them here.

There are also breeds of cats once known in the United States but no longer to be seen here. One of these was the Australian cat, which was not really Australian at all. It was, or so it is generally believed, a mutation of the Siamese breed which was introduced into Australia. It came to this country by way of England. The cat, of varying colors, had very short fur, little or no whiskers, big ears, and a pointed head with a long nose. It was seen a good deal at cat shows a half century ago.

Another breed that has vanished from the American scene is the Mexican hairless cat (sometimes called, rather chauvinistically, the New Mexican hairless cat). In all candor, it must be said that this is a loss that can be borne, for the hairless cat was surely one of the strangest—and ugliest—creatures ever bred. It looked somewhat like a cross of a cat and a rat. It apparently began as a mutation, which then was cultivated. It had big ears, a bare tail, and a hide like that of a boxer dog.

Today, in the United States, there are roughly forty recognized breeds. I say "roughly" because the various show-sanctioning associations do not agree with each other entirely on this matter of breed recognition. This lack of agreement and coordination is unfortunate. In Great Britain the Governing Council of the Cat Fancy is the single, supreme authority for English catdom. In this country, uniformity is maintained in the dog fancy by the American Kennel Club. But the cat fancy here is ruled by six different stud-book organizations, at last count, and it sometimes gets a little confusing.

In the following pages we shall discuss all the breeds that are recognized by any of the American cat fanciers' associations. This list is divided into two major groups according to coat: long-hair and short-hair. It should be noted, however, that there is a third coat type—the rex. This is a wavy, or kinky, coat that occurs as a mutation. It has also been found in the rabbit and the mouse. Some British breeders are trying to develop the rex type of coat as a true-breeding strain in cats, but they have found some indications that the rex is not a single kind of coat, but that several different types have been given this name. In time, it is likely that the rex will be a cat as fully developed in its breeding as the breeds that we shall now describe.

LONG-HAIRS

The origin of the long-haired cats has long been the subject of fascinated speculation by cat fanciers. The type could have been developed through selective breeding, beginning with mutants. The Tibetan temple cat, for instance, probably came into being this way, its long coat being peculiarly suitable to the cold climate in which these cats lived.

Many zoologists, on the other hand, are inclined to wonder whether the manul, also known as Pallas' cat, might not have been one of the ancestors of the long-hairs. The manul, about the size of a domestic cat, is a beautiful creature. It has very long, fine hair, faintly dotted on a ground of grayish-brown. It has side-whiskers that are not as prominent as those of a lynx. It is found from the Caspian Sea to Tibet, and north to Siberia, but always in the mountains and the high plains, where the temperature is low.

The Caspian Sea, of course, is the northern frontier of Iran, ancient Persia, and it is close to Turkey, whose capital, Ankara, used to be called Angora. And the long-haired cats were, until fairly recently, called Angoras and Persians.

It is generally assumed now that Angora and Persian were simply different names for the same type of cats, but this is not correct. A half century ago Helen Winslow, writing about the long-hairs of her day, specifically mentioned the differences between the two breeds, although it was only a few more years until another cat fancier, Frances Simpson, was obliged to write, "The distinctions between Angoras and Persians are of so fine a nature that I must be pardoned if I ignore the class of cat commonly called Angora which seems gradually to have disappeared from our midst."

What were the differences between the two breeds? The face of the Persian was round, the nose short and broad, the ears short, and the eyes large and round. The Angora, on the other hand, had a wedge-shaped head, a muzzle that was not the least bit stubby, medium-sized ears, and eyes that might be round but often were slightly slanted. The Angora's fur was long and silky, while the Persian's was somewhat coarse.

When Angoras and Persians were bred together, as they often were, the Angora characteristics tended to disappear and the Persian dominated.

Recently, however, some cats have been carried from Turkey to England, where they have excited a good deal of comment. They appear to be true Angoras of the type not seen in the Western world for many years. Perhaps the Angora may make a comeback yet.

The standard* for the long-hairs makes these specifications:

TYPE: The perfect cat should be of cobby type; that is to say, low on the legs, deep in the chest, massive across the shoulders and rump, with a short, well-rounded middle piece. In size the cat should be large or medium, but there should be no sacrifice of quality for the sake of mere size.

HEAD: The head should be round and massive, with great breadth of skull, and be well set on a neck not too long.

EARS: Neat, round-tipped, set far apart, and not unduly open at the base.

NOSE: Short, snub, and broad.

CHEEKS: Full.

JAWS: Broad and powerful.

EYES: Large, round, full, set far apart and brilliant, giving a sweet expression to the face.

TAIL: Short, carried without a curve and at an angle lower than the back, but not trailed when walking.

BACK: Level.

LEGS: Thick and strong forelegs, perfectly straight.

---

* The *standard* of a breed is a description of the perfect specimen; thus, the standard serves as a means of evaluating a given cat. All long-haired cats, apart from coat color, have the same standard, except for the Peke-faced. The standards for short-haired cats, as will be evident later in this chapter, show considerable variation in conformation from breed to breed.

PAWS: Large, round, and firm; toes carried close, five in front and four behind.

COAT: Long hair. The coat should show primarily perfect physical condition. It should be of fine texture, soft, glossy, full of life, and should stand off from the body. It should be long all over the body, including the shoulders. The ruff should be immense and continue in a deep frill between the front legs. Ear tufts, long, curved. Toe tufts, long. Brush very full.

UNDESIRABLE: Rangy, flat-sided, narrow-chested, long, spindle-legged, long-tailed cats, with long noses, large ears, pointed and upright eyes set bias or close together, receding chin, light bone, a general "foxy" face, slant eyes, Roman nose.

This is the description of the long-hairs that establishes the aims of the breeders. It cannot, of course, picture the personality of these cats very well.

Those who do not fancy the long-hairs assert that they are less intelligent than the short-hairs, less easily trained, less companionable. But say that to an admirer of long-hairs and you'll find yourself in quite a little cat fight. The truth is, obviously, that there are cats and there are cats—and that your cat, as often as not, will display about as much intelligence as it finds necessary.

There have been fabulously clever long-hairs that did all manner of tricks, and there have been long-hairs that didn't know enough to show up for dinner. Intelligence is where you find it.

Probably one reason why some people dislike long-hairs is that the humans feel inferior. Long-hairs have a way of making some people feel that way. They look as luxurious and elegant as any creature that ever walked the earth, and the expression on their faces betrays their firm conviction that they are slumming when they're visiting you.

This isn't always true, of course. A lovely long-hair named Cleo will always remain a vivid, charming memory in the minds of everyone who ever met her. She was beautiful and feminine and as silly as a cat could be—but always in a dignified way. She would leap gracefully from a chair to a table, but she always somehow misjudged the distance, so the graceful arc of her body through the air would end when her nose bashed into the edge of the table. And then there were the times when she tried to walk, and became bewildered by the difficulty of it all; someone was standing on her tail, and the someone was Cleo herself!

A long-haired cat carries with it special responsibilities for its owner because of its special grooming needs, but this will be discussed in a later chapter.

The long-hairs are divided according to color. These are the colors:

White: Pure white, no colored hairs; eyes deep blue or deep orange. Winners to be withheld for blue-eyed whites showing a clearly defined area of copper in one or both eyes, and from copper-eyed whites showing a clearly defined area of blue in one or both eyes. (At least one show standard, however, says that the cat may have one blue and one orange eye; such a cat is called, appropriately, an odd-eyed white long-hair.)

White cats have a tendency to deafness, and this is particularly true of blue-eyed whites, but breeders have been working steadily toward the development of whites without this defect, with some success. Blue-eyed whites are also somewhat difficult to breed, so they are less commonly encountered than most other cats. On the other hand, white cats—long- or short-haired—often are born with green eyes; these cats are lovely but they are not recognized as a breed by the authorities, and they cannot be shown in competition.

Black: Dense coal black, sound from roots to tip of fur, absolutely free from any tinge of rust on tips or smoke in undercoat. Eyes copper or deep orange.

It is unusual to find a black whose color is true. As a kitten, the black often looks badly off-color, sometimes to the extent of being rust-brown. Until the kitten is more than six months old, one can't be sure whether its color will clear or remain faulty.

Moreover, the adult black, even if it be, as the English standard puts it, "lustrous raven black to the roots," can be bleached to a washed-out shade by a strong sun—a consideration which must be borne in mind by anyone who is thinking of exhibiting a black.

The blacks are one of the oldest long-hairs, and legend has it that they were once the exclusive property of the Shah of Iran, who bestowed them on his favorites.

Blue: Color blue, not drab, lighter shade preferred, one level tone, without shading or marking from nose to tip of tail, and sound to the roots. Eyes brilliant copper or deep orange.

UNDESIRABLE: Pale yellow eyes. Winners to be withheld for green eyes.

This is an uncommonly handsome and deservedly popular long-hair, but somewhat tricky to breed, for white, black, and brown tabby all dominate the blue factor. It is not uncommon for a kitten of this breed to display tabby markings, but these usually fade away completely by the time it is a full-grown cat.

Red: Deep, rich, clear, brilliant red without shading, markings, or ticking, lips and chin same color as coat. Eyes brilliant copper or deep orange. Markings or bars undesirable.

This is a rare long-hair, possibly the rarest, and a cat that is very difficult to breed. A few are exhibited in this country and in parts of Europe, but the British fanciers have openly challenged the validity of even those few; it is almost unheard-of for an all-red long-hair to be shown there. Part of the difficulty lies in the persistence of the red's ancestor, the red tabby: the tabby stripes tend to come through, even though faintly, in most of the cats that appear to be all-red. And if the stripes don't appear, some of the characteristic rings on the tail are almost certain to show up. All of which is a pity, for this is a marvelous cat.

Cream: One level shade of cream, sound to the roots. Eyes brilliant copper or deep orange.

This breed, curiously, is believed to have been produced initially by the crossing of a red tabby with a tortoiseshell, because the latter has in its coat the cream factor, as well as black and red. In this breed, too, the kittens may well show a certain amount of striping on the legs or tail, but this usually clears before the cat is adult.

Chinchilla (Silver): The undercoat should be pure white, the coat on back, flanks, head, and tail being sufficiently tipped with black to give the characteristic sparkling silver appearance; the legs may be very slightly shaded with the tipping, but chin, ear tufts, stomach, and chest must be pure white. Any barring or brown or cream tinge is a fault. Eyes to be green or blue-green. Rims of eyes, lips, and nose to be outlined with black. Center of nose to be a brick red.

This is essentially the same breed as the following one.

Shaded Silver: Should be pure, unmarked silver, shading gradually down the sides, face, and tail, from dark on the ridge to white on chin, chest, and belly and under the tail; the legs to be the same tone as the face. The general effect to be much darker than a chinchilla. Any barring or brown or cream tinge to be considered a fault. Eyes to be green or blue-green. Rims of eyes, lips, and nose to be outlined with black. Center of nose to be brick red.

The shaded silver is, essentially, a very heavily ticked chinchilla. The name "chinchilla" is more than a little misleading, for these cats do not in any way resemble the tiny fur-bearing animal of the Andes or the chinchilla variety of rabbit; the best one can say is that all these animals, including the cats, have some shade of gray on most of their bodies.

These are among the most magnificent of long-hairs, but the kittens almost always display the tabby bars and stripes. These fade away as the cat grows up, and often the kitten that was most sharply marked emerges as the cat with no trace of tabby at all.

Smoke: Should appear black with white undercoat and black points and mask, light silver frill and ear tufts. (The British standard permits blue instead of black in the coat color.) Eyes to be brilliant copper or deep orange (also described in some American standards as: golden to copper.)

UNDESIRABLE: White spots or hairs or black locket, gray topcoat or dingy undercoat, marked shading or bars. No tabby markings allowed.

"The cat of contrasts" is the name often bestowed on this breed.

The dark mask and points contrast pleasantly with the frill and the ear tufts. The kittens are born black, or sometimes a rusty kind of half-black, and it is not until they are a few weeks old that the pale hairs of the undercoat begin to make their appearance. Cats of this breed are rather uncommon today.

Silver Tabby: Color should be a pale clear silver with broad, dense black markings clearly defined and broad (not narrow pencilings). Legs evenly barred, "bracelets" coming up high to meet the body markings. Tail barred. Barring on neck and chest, or "necklaces," distinct, like so many chains. Head barred. Cheek swirls and swirls on the side of body, each continuing in an unbroken ring. The marks upon the face, between the ears and down the neck to meet the "butterfly" on the shoulders, which divides the head lines from the spine line. Back markings to consist of a distinct black stripe down the middle of the back with stripes of the ground color on either side of it, and black lines on either side of them. No ticking.

UNDESIRABLE FOR ALL TABBIES: Indistinct or wrong markings. Lips and chin to be the same shade as the rings around the eyes. Any brown or cream tinge in the ground color to be considered a fault. Eye color green or hazel—green preferred. (Some American standards call for blue-green eyes.)

The tabby may be said to be the basic domestic cat. It is the most commonly seen variety of alley cat, and it clearly goes back to the wild cat ancestors of the household pet. The tabbies, as we have already mentioned, occur in two forms, the striped and the blotched, but only the striped is acceptable for exhibition. And these striped cats have been developed, through breeding, to a point where the stripes conform to a definite and true-breeding pattern. The symmetry of these cats is a miracle too often taken for granted, even by cat fanciers.

Genetically, the tabby factor is dominant to everything but white, so it is little wonder that the tabbies are so common.

Brown Tabby: Ground color any shade of true brown which has no grayish tinge and which affords good contrast with the markings;

brilliant coppery brown preferred. Markings to conform with those described for silver tabby. Allowances to be made for light chins in kittens and young adults. Eyes copper or deep orange, copper preferred.

The light chin is a dominant in the heredity of the brown tabby, but it is being bred out of these cats. As with all the other tabbies except the red, the kittens of this breed are difficult to distinguish as to show quality, for the tabby markings are indistinct and ill-defined at first.

Blue Tabby: Ground color, including lips and chin, pale bluish ivory, with warm fawn overtones; fawn more noticeable on upper part of face. Markings very deep blue affording good contrast with ground color. Pattern of markings as described for silver tabby. Lips and chin slightly lighter in kittens and young adults. Nose leather rose. Eyes copper or deep orange, copper preferred.

The British, and many of the American cat fanciers' associations do not recognize the blue tabby. It is an extremely attractive cat, as you may well imagine.

Red Tabby: Ground color, including lips and chin area, red, markings as described for silver tabby and to be a deep rich red. No ticking. Eyes copper or deep orange.

Sometimes called the orange tabby, this cat is seen in its pet (as opposed to show) form as the "marmalade" or "ginger" cat. But the color in the pet ginger tends to sand, whereas the red tabby's coat is a rich, vivid color.

It will be noted that the blue and the red tabbies are color on color (blue on blue in the one cat, red on red in the other), unlike the silver and brown tabbies, in which the coat is black on color.

One difficulty in breeding red tabbies is the white tip which tends to show up on the tail. Cats with this fault should never be used in breeding. On the other hand, red tabbies have one helpful quality: the markings are sharp and clear in the kitten, so the best show prospects can be chosen at an early age.

Tortoiseshell: Black, orange, and cream, bright, clearly defined, and well broken even to the feet. Patched, not brindled.

DESIRABLE: Half of nose black, half orange, known as the "blaze." No tabby markings. Eyes copper or deep orange.

UNDESIRABLE: Brindled colors.

Add one color, and one gets the next breed.

Tortoiseshell-and-White (Calico): Three colors, black, red, and cream, to be well distributed, clearly patched, and interspersed with white. White should be in distinct, predominant areas on chest, face, legs, and paws. White blaze is desirable. Eyes brilliant copper or deep orange.

UNDESIRABLE: Blending of colors, brindling, white hairs in colored patches, tabby markings, and black feet.

In these two particolored breeds, solid color on face, legs, or tail is a serious fault.

Males are extremely rare in both of these breeds, as well as in the next breed, the blue-cream. They occur perhaps once in a million births (the ratio is pure guess, and probably conservative). But when males are produced, they are almost always sterile. One or two male tortoiseshell and calico cats have actually grown up to sire kittens. I know of no blue-cream male, however, which has ever grown beyond kittenhood. For those readers who may be wondering what conceivable connection there can be between the tortoiseshell and the blue-cream, it is worth mentioning here that geneticists describe the blue-cream of cats as the dilution of black and red, a dilution being the reduction of color caused by a scarcity of pigment granules. It has been said that the genetic phenomenon seen in these three breeds is the only known example of sex-linkage in mammals except for the sex-linked defects in man, such as hemophilia and baldness.

Because of this sex-linkage, it follows that tortoiseshells and calicoes with the proper size and distribution of patterns cannot be bred to order; they happen. And so there are relatively few of them that measure up to the standard for the breed.

They happen, theoretically, when cats of the three colors indicated are bred together, that is, a cream male is mated with a red female, and a female offspring of that union is bred to a black male. In practice, this seldom works out, because so many other genetic factors are at work at the same time. But carry out this breeding plan consistently, and tortoiseshells should result. Carry it one step further, and a calico should be produced.

Here is one tortoiseshell breeding plan*:

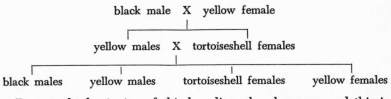

Reverse the beginning of this breeding plan, however, and this is the result:

If this seems rather bewilderingly complicated, it is. But a rudimentary knowledge of this unusual breeding problem is essential to anyone who wants to learn about cats.

Blue-Cream: The two colors, blue and cream, well-divided and broken into patches on body, face, and feet; bright and well-defined. No ticking. Eyes brilliant copper or deep orange.

UNDESIRABLE: Colors brindled rather than broken, solid color on face, legs, or tail.

The genetic peculiarities of this breed have been discussed above

* This chart is based on material in A. C. Jude's invaluable book, *Cat Genetics* (All-Pets Books, Inc., Fond du Lac, Wisconsin, 1955), to which cat fanciers interested in breeding problems should refer.

in the commentary on the tortoiseshell and the tortoiseshell-and-white breeds, and needn't be repeated here. The following breeding patterns in blue-creams might be of interest, however:

Blue females bred with blue males produce blue females and blue males.

Blue females × cream males = blue-cream females and blue males.

Blue-cream females × blue males = blue females, blue-cream females, blue males, and cream males.

Blue-cream females × cream males = blue-cream females, cream females, blue males, and cream males.

Cream females × blue males = blue-cream females and cream males.

Cream females × cream males = cream females and cream males.

Because of the breeding difficulties, blue-creams are not often seen.

Shell Cameo: The undercoat should be a pale cream, practically white. The coat on the back, flanks, head and tail should be sufficiently tipped with red to give a delicate tinsel appearance. The face and legs may be very slightly shaded with tipping, but the chin, ear tufts, stomach, and chest should be practically white, without tipping. Eyes gold or copper and the rims of eyes and nose leather rose.

The cameos—there are now four of them (the others appear below) —are among the newest of the breeds. Dr. Rachel Salisbury has been credited with originating this color. In *Cats Magazine* of February, 1961, she wrote this brief account of its origin:

"It was first developed intensively and deliberately at Wanaki Cattery, in Milton Junction, Wisconsin. Although over a period of twenty-odd years the owner had noted 'pink' male kittens in various litters from a smoke-tortie crossing, she did not settled down to serious development of the color until 1954. The color, called cameo because of the effect of its combination of cream and red, has now been standardized to the fifth generation—although third-generation cameos will breed true every time."

The development of the cameos has been extremely rapid. By May, 1959, just five years after earnest cultivation of the breed began, the Cameo Cat Club of America was organized.

These are creatures of an almost unearthly, fragile beauty, and they should quickly win a following among those who love cats.

Shaded Cameo: Pure, unmarked red, with definite gradual shading down the sides, face, and tail from dark on the ridge to whitish cream on the chin, chest, stomach, and under the tail. Legs to be the same tone as the face. The general effect should be much redder than the shell cameo. Eyes gold or copper and nose leather and rims of eyes rose.

Smoke Cameo: Should appear to be a deep reddish beige, with white or well-contrasted cream undercoat, red or deep beige points, and mask with white or pale cream neck ruff and ear tufts. Eyes gold or copper.

UNDESIRABLE FOR SHELL, SHADED, AND SMOKE CAMEO: Barring on face, legs, body, and tail; trace of green, blue, or pale yellow in eyes; black rims on eyes and nose leather.

Tabby Cameo: The ground color of pale cream should be broken with well-defined red or beige tabby markings. Eyes gold or copper.

UNDESIRABLE: Trace of blue, green, or pale yellow in eyes; black rims on eyes and nose leather.

Peke-Faced: Should conform in color, markings, and general type to the standards set forth for the red and the red tabby long-haired cats. The head should resemble as much as possible that of the Pekinese dog from which it gets its name. The nose should be very short and depressed, or indented, between the eyes. There should be a decidedly wrinkled muzzle. Eyes should be very round, large, and full, set wide apart, prominent and brilliant. Irregularities of teeth and underjaw frequently found in the Peke are objectionable, as are also ears set close together and upright.

This breed was recognized to take in those red and red tabby long-hairs that began to produce heavy-jowled offspring. By 1938 there was at least one Peke-faced champion in the United States. The breed is not recognized abroad.

Himalayan: Type and conformation the same as for other long-hairs. Color and points the same as for Siamese, with the same color classes. Eyes blue, the deeper the better.

UNDESIRABLE: Any similarity in conformation to Siamese. Eyes any color other than blue. Winners to be withheld for kinked tails, crossed eyes, or white toes.

This is another new breed, and one which has excited much favorable comment by visitors to recent cat shows. In Great Britain this breed is called the *colorpoint* long-hair.

Before World War II Mrs. Virginia R. Cobb and Dr. Clyde E. Keeler conducted some genetic experiments with Siamese cats. These included crossing the Siamese with long-hairs. The Siamese color proved recessive. On the other hand, the short hair appeared dominant over the long hair. The kittens all took their color from the long-haired parent and their type of coat from the Siamese parent. By mating the kittens to each other, however, the experimenters were able to produce a cat that was, essentially, a long-haired Siamese.

The experiments were then abandoned, to the relief of Siamese fanciers, including Brian A. Stirling-Webb of England, who regarded the entire matter as nothing less than a desecration of their breed. In 1947, however, Stirling-Webb came across a stray long-hair that was Siamese in coloring but a true Persian in type. This was quite another matter from the "long-haired Siamese." Stirling-Webb was so taken by the beauty of the stray that he began breeding experiments to try to develop such a cat.

About the same time, in America, Marguerita Goforth, having seen the mixed Siamese-long-hair pet of a friend, began to wonder about the possibilities of developing a strain of true long-hairs with Siamese coloring. She knew nothing about Stirling-Webb's work, and he was unaware of hers. In 1955 the Governing Council of the Cat Fancy recognized Stirling-Webb's cats, which had now produced the third true-breeding generation, as a new breed. Two years later the Goforth first list of Himalayans was recognized by one of the American associations, soon followed by the other organizations.

The American cats of this breed were named Himalayans not because they came from that mountain range—they didn't—but because the color pattern is similar to that of the Himalayan rabbit.

The Himalayans are a little more active than other long-hairs, but have the gentle voice of the Persian, not the loud and imperative voice of the Siamese.

SHORT-HAIRS

The short-haired cats include breeds which differ from each other to a far greater degree than the long-haired breeds, most of which are basically only color variations of the same foundation breed, the Persian. The short-haired breeds each have their own unique qualities which make them quite distinct in the short-hair division—as different from each other as they are from the long-hairs.

Domestic Short-Hair

HEAD: Broad, with cheeks especially well developed in studs. Nose and face medium short with eyes set wide apart. Muzzle should present a squarish aspect but should not be as short as in the long-hairs.

EARS: Medium in size, rounded at tips, wide set and not too large at the base.

EYES: Round, full, set to show breadth of nose.

CHIN: Well-developed, forming a perpendicular line with the upper lip.

NECK: Medium short and denoting strength; should be in proportion to the body.

BODY: Well-knit and powerful, showing good depth of body, full chest, and ranging from medium to large in size.

TAIL: Slightly heavy at base, tapering to an abrupt end; in proportion to the body.

LEGS AND FEET: Legs of good substance; in proportion to the body. Not too high on legs. Feet neat and well-rounded.

COAT: Short, thick, even in texture, well-bodied, giving a general appearance of shortness. Somewhat heavier and thicker during winter months.

COLOR: Requirements for color of coat and eye color the same as for long-haired cats.

CONDITION: Hard and muscular, giving a general appearance of strength and vigor.

BALANCE: All physical aspects of the cat should complement one another to present a perfect picture.

UNDESIRABLE: Too high on legs, receding chin, snub nose or Peke face, too fine or fluffy coat, long nose or wedge-shaped head, long pointed ears or ears set too close, narrow slanting eye or Oriental look, neck too short and thick or too long and slender, tail too short or whiplike. The domestic short-hair should not resemble the Siamese in any manner.

"Democratic" is the word that domestic short-hair breeders have bestowed, like a ribbon, on their cats, and it is a fitting adjective. After all, a cat doesn't acquire special virtue simply because it originated in a foreign country. These cats are easy to get, and often difficult to avoid. And they are as easy to love as they are to get, for they have intelligence, character, liveliness, ingenuity, and a sensible irreverence toward pomp and ceremony. The show cats of this breed have been carefully bred and cultivated for generations, and they are the worthy elite of American cats.

Siamese

COLOR: Siamese cats shall be known as Seal Points, Blue Points, Chocolate Points, Lilac Points, and Albinos. (See also Red Colorpoint Short-Hair later in this chapter.)

BODY COLOR: In judging older cats, allowances should be made for darker coats, since Siamese generally darken with age, but there should be a definite contrast between body color and points.

POINTS: Mask, ears, legs, feet and tail, dense and clearly defined, all of the same shade. Mask should be connected to the ears by tracings except in kittens.

COAT: Short, fine in texture, glossy, lying close to the body.

CONDITION: Good physical condition, not fat, inclined to muscle. Judges to penalize for emaciation.

HEAD: Head should be long and should taper in a fine wedge from ears to narrow muzzle, with no whisker break. The receding chin caused by failure of the upper and lower teeth to meet in a straight line shall be considered a serious fault. The skull is to be flat, and the nose is to be a continuation of the forehead with no break. In profile, a straight line is to be seen from the center of the forehead to the tip of the nose. Allowance is to be made for jowls in a stud cat. There should be the width of an eye between the eyes. Ears rather large and pricked wide at the base; they should continue the line of the wedge.

BODY TYPE: The body should be medium in size, dainty, long, and svelte. Males to be proportionately larger than females. Neck long and slender. Legs proportionately long and slim; hind legs slightly higher than the front. Feet small and oval in shape. Tail long and tapering with no visible kinks.

EYES: Eye aperture almond-shaped and slanting toward the nose in true oriental fashion.

UNDESIRABLE FOR ALL SIAMESE: Rounded head, fat, thick-set specimens. Hood (a continuation or an extension of the point coloring over the top of the head, around the sides, and under the throat; the mask, instead of fading away gradually at the throat, makes a distinct change in color so it would appear that a hood was tied around the head; tracings to the ears are lost as the mask continues up between the ears). Rough shaggy coats. Odd eye color; gray or yellowish tinge in eyes, crossed eyes. Belly and hip spots. Tabby and ticked markings. Light hairs in the points. White feet or toes. Receding chin. Kink in tail.

Seal Point: Color, even pale fawn to cream, shading gradually into a lighter color on the stomach and chest. The coat color should not be gray. Points all the same shade of deep seal brown. Eyes should be clear and of a vivid deep blue color. Pads of feet and nose leather the same color as the points.

Blue Point: Coat color is to be a bluish white on the stomach and chest. Points should be all the same shade of definite blue giving strong contrast of divided color. There must be no fawn in the coat. Pads of feet and nose leather to be slate colored. Eyes clear and as deep blue as possible within the breed.

Chocolate Point: Body color ivory all over. Points milk chocolate color. Gray or dingy shading on the body is a fault. Pads of feet and nose leather a cinnamon-pink color. Eyes clear and as deep blue as possible within the breed. Pale or slatey eyes to be discouraged.

Lilac Point: Body color to be glacial white. Points frosty gray with pinkish tone. Pads of feet and nose leather mauve. Eye color clear and as deep blue as possible for the breed. Pale or slatey eyes to be discouraged.

Albino: Body color to be a white which is not chalky and dull. The coat has a true Siamese sheen and is short and close-lying. The eye color is not the pink of white rabbits because the blue of the blood vessels and muscles shows through to some extent.

One of the most unexpected facts about the Siamese cat is that it is not the common cat of Siam (Thailand) and probably was not originally native to that country. Indeed, in the country for which it is named the natives often call it "the Chinese cat." Nothing is dependable in this world.

The Siamese cat undoubtedly originated as a mutation somewhere in the Far East. Siamese royalty, attracted by the unusual and attractive color patterns, bought all of these cats that could be found, at inflated prices, and proceeded to breed them. By 1830, at the latest, the breed was well established in Thailand.

In 1884 the Siamese royal family gave two of the cats to the British Resident in Bangkok, Owen Gould, who took them home with him and exhibited them at a cat show the following year in London. They aroused so much interest that several other pairs were imported to England in the next few years. About 1895 the first Siamese were imported into the United States, where they took hold immediately. For more than a quarter of a century there have been more Siamese cats in this country than in Thailand.

From a breeder's point of view, these cats have a couple of faults that must be guarded against carefully: a kink in the tail (common to many of the cats from southeast Asia) and crossed eyes. From a pet owner's point of view, they have one serious drawback: their

51

fondness for "talking"—meowing in a clear, high, articulate voice that is unlike the call of any other breed except the Burmese. It is a sound that can be somewhat nerve-wracking after a while.

But this is a small price to pay for the pleasure of sharing one's home with a Siamese cat, one of the most playful, gay, intelligent, companionable, and affectionate of all cats—indeed, of all animals. Siamese not only love to talk, they love to listen, too, to take part in conversations. They are mischievous and clever and curious. They quickly become a part of one's family.

A breed very closely related to the Siamese is the Burmese. As Sinnott, Dunn, and Dobzhansky (see Bibliography) have pointed out, "one of the alleles [alternate forms of the genes] of the albino series gives the so-called Siamese color highly prized by cat fanciers." The Burmese, too, belong to this albino series. Phyllis Lauder says that Burmese is dominant to Siamese, and two cats both carrying genes for Burmese and Siamese will produce three Burmese kittens to one Siamese—the Mendelian 3:1 ratio.

All of this will be of little interest to the average cat lover. It is cited here only as an illustration of the extremely close family connection between the Siamese and the Burmese.

Now let us look at these Burmese.

Burmese

DEFINITION: The overall impression of the ideal Burmese would be a cat of medium size and rich solid color; with substantial bone structure, good muscular development, and a surprising weight for its apparent size. This, together with its expressive eyes and sweet face, presents a totally distinctive cat which is comparable to no other breed.

COLOR: The mature specimen should be a rich, warm, sable brown, shading almost imperceptibly to a slightly lighter hue on the underparts, but otherwise without shadings or markings of any kind. Allowance should be made for a lighter color and possibly faint striping in adolescents and kittens. White spots or patches disqualify.

BODY AND TAIL: Body medium in size, muscular in development, and presenting a compact appearance. Allowance should be made for larger size in males. An ample, rounded chest, with back level from shoulder to tail. Legs well proportioned to body, with round feet. Tail to be straight, medium in length, slightly tapering, and free from visible defects.

HEAD AND EARS: The head should be pleasingly rounded and without flat planes, whether viewed from front or side. Face should be full, with considerable breadth between the eyes, tapering slightly to a short, well-developed muzzle. In profile there should be a visible nose break. Ears to be medium in size and set well apart on a rounded skull; alert, tilting slightly forward, broad at base with slightly rounded tips.

EYES: Set far apart with round aperture, with color ranging from yellow to gold; the greater the depth and brilliance the better.

COAT: Fine, glossy, satinlike texture; very close-lying.

CONDITION: Perfect physical condition with excellent muscle tone. There should be no evidence of obesity, paunchiness, weakness, or apathy.

UNDESIRABLE: Pale eye color; green or odd eyes; tabby markings. Winners to be withheld from cats with bobbed, screw, kinked, or pom-pom tails, or blue eyes.

Somewhat smaller than the typical Siamese, the Burmese is a superb, richly colored cat, lithe, playful, very affectionate, unafraid, and gentle. In 1930 Dr. Joseph C. Thompson of San Francisco imported the first Burmese cat into the United States. In the late 1950's this breed began to attract an increasing amount of attention.

Abyssinian

COLOR AND TICKING: Color: ruddy brown, ticked with various shades of darker brown or black. Darker shading along spine allowed if fully ticked. The underside and forelegs (inside) to be a tint to harmonize with the main body color; undersides and inside forelegs to show no more ticking than a single band of darker color at the tip of hair, preference given to unmarked orange-brown (burnt sienna) color. Nose leather tile red. Paw pads black with black extending beyond the paws of the hind legs. Ticking: evenly ticked with double or triple bands of color on each hair over saddle, sides, chest and tail, without patching or irregularity.

BODY AND TAIL: Body medium long, lithe and graceful, but showing well-developed muscular strength. Legs proportionately slim, fine-boned, with feet small, round, neat and compact. When standing, the cat should give the impression of being on tiptoe. Tail thick at the base, fairly long and tapering, tipped with black. Abyssinian conformation strikes a medium between the extremes of the cobby and the svelte lengthy type. General balance more to be desired than mere size alone.

HEAD AND EARS: Head should show a modified, slightly rounded wedge without flat planes, the brow, cheek, and profile lines all showing a gentle contour. A slight rise from the bridge of the nose to the forehead; forehead of good size with width between the ears and flowing into the arched neck without a break. Muzzle not sharply pointed. Allowance to be made for jowls in the males. Ears alert, large and pointed, broad at base, preferably tipped with black or brown. Hair on ears very short and close-lying. Inner ear bare and open.

EYES: Almond-shaped, large, brilliant, and expressive. Skull aperture follows almond shape of eyes; that is, neither round nor oriental. Color: gold, green, or hazel, the more depth and richness the better.

COAT: Soft, silky, fine in texture, but dense and resilient to the touch, with a lustrous sheen. Medium in length but long enough to accommodate two or three bands of ticking separated by lighter bands.

CONDITION: Lithe, hard, and muscular, giving the appearance of activity, sound health, and general vigor.

UNDESIRABLE: Bars, rings, tabby markings, or unbroken necklace. White, other than nostril, chin, and upper throat area, is a serious fault. Locket, unbroken necklace. Coldness or gray tones in color. Cobby or rangy body; scanty, whip, or abnormal tail; short heavy legs; splayed or pointed feet; round head; small ears; pale or small eyes; coarse, thin, or long coat.

The Abyssinian has one thing in common with the Burmese and the Siamese—there is doubt that it is a native of the country whose

THE BREEDS

name it carries. It is said authoritatively that there was no native breed in Abyssinia (Ethiopia). On the other hand, the Abyssinian cat looks very much like the domestic cat of the ancient Egyptians. It appears to be closely derived from two African wild cats, *Felis lybica* and *Felis ocreata*. There is no reason to believe that such a domesticated cat would not have been kept as a household pet in Abyssinia.

One thing is known: the first Abyssinian in the Western world was taken to Great Britain in 1869 by an English army officer's wife who had obtained it in Abyssinia. So perhaps the authorities are wrong.

The Abyssinian is an exotic-looking, active, very friendly cat.

Russian Blue

COLOR: Bright blue, even throughout and, in maturity, free from tabby markings and shadings. There are various shades of blue, but the lighter or lavender blue is preferred. No white permissible.

COAT: The fur should be very short, thick, and very fine, standing up soft and silky like sealskin. Very different fur from that of any other breed of cat. It should not lie flat. The coat should be double so that the coat has a distinct sheen. The texture and appearance of the coat is the truest criterion of the Russian blue.

BODY AND TAIL: Body, fine in bone, long, lithe, and graceful outline, and carriage with tail fairly long and tapering. Legs should be longer than those of the domestic short-hair, and the feet should be small, neat, and well-rounded.

HEAD AND NECK: Skull should be flat. Face should be broad across the eyes; it looks wide because of the heavy fur. The nose is longer than that of the Persian but shorter than that of the Siamese. The neck is fairly long but looks short because of the thick fur.

EYES: Set rather wide apart, round, and in maturity as vivid green in color as possible. Kittens and adolescent cats have yellow eyes.

EARS: Rather large, wide at the base, pointed at the tips rather than round, and with very little inside furnishings. Skin of ears thin and not too thickly covered with hair.

This is the alley cat of Russia, which was often called the "Archangel cat" by British sailors who carried it home on their ships from that Northern port. Or perhaps one should say that this is one of the theories to account for this handsome beast.

"Maltese" is another, now passé, name sometimes bestowed on this cat. Since Malta is a long way from Russia, it would seem that there is a certain amount of confusion surrounding the question of this cat's origin.

Regardless of its origin, however, the Russian cat is an uncommonly graceful, courageous, noble animal whose loyalty must be experienced to be believed. The Russian blue is scarcely ever seen these days.

British Blue

COLOR: Light to medium blue, very even and without tabby markings or shadings. No white.

COAT: Short and thick, but without cottony texture of Russian blue.

FORM: Compact build with fairly short legs, tail thick at base, medium length, but not tapering. Head round and broad. Ears small and well-rounded at tips.

EYES: Large and full. Orange, yellow, or copper. Green tinge not allowed.

CONDITION: Body very firm and fairly fat.

These cats, somewhat more full-faced than the Russian blues, a little cobbier, and generally with a no-nonsense, eminently British look about them, are, unfortunately, almost never seen in the United States anymore. It's a pity; these cats should be able to earn a real following.

Manx

COLOR AND MARKINGS: All colors of Manx are recognized, including ticked and mackerel tabbies and particolored. Winners are not to be withheld for white "buttons" or "lockets."

COAT: Should be of good texture, with a well-padded quality arising from the longer, open, outer coat and the thicker and closer undercoat, known as a double coat.

BODY: Should be solid, compact, and well-balanced, with the back showing a definite incline from the shoulders to the haunches, resulting from the back legs being longer than the front legs. In size, the Manx should be small or medium and "bunnylike" in appearance. Males may be larger, but not rangy.

DEPTH OF FLANK: The flank, on the Manx cat, should be of much greater depth than that of any other breed, adding to the cobbiness and balance of the perfect Manx type.

TAILLESSNESS: Must be absolute in a perfect specimen. There should be a decided hollow at the end of the backbone where, in the ordinary cat, a tail would begin. Sometimes there is a rise of bone at the end of the spine; this is a fault and should be penalized, but should not cause disqualification. In an otherwise perfect or exceptional specimen, an invisible joint or cartilage will be allowed, but penalized. Winners to be withheld from all other stumpies (all Manx with definite visible joints).

SHORTNESS OF BACK: Back should be sturdy and short, so as to conform with the actual size of the well-balanced Manx cat.

LEGS AND FEET: Legs should be of good substance, with the front legs short and well set apart to show good depth of chest, while the back legs are much longer with a heavy, muscular thigh, tapering down to a substantial lower leg. This lower leg often has the hair worn off due to the fact that the Manx rests on this part as often as on the paws. Feet should be small, neat, and well-rounded, with five toes in front and four toes on the back legs.

HEAD AND EARS: Head should be fairly round with prominent cheeks (jowly appearance); muzzle should taper but not to a sharp point, so as to give the appearance of snippiness, resulting from a pinch or whisker break. The head longer than that of a domestic short-hair and without a decided nose break. Ears rather wide at base, tapering slightly to a point and longer than those of a domestic short-hair, but in proportion to the head.

EYES: Large, round, and full; color standard according to color of coat as in other breeds. Points to be divided equally between size and color.

CONDITION: Good physical condition. Muscular; good flesh, but not fat.

UNDESIRABLE: Flat-sided, narrow-chested cats with front legs that are too high, thin legs, or weak or receding chins. Manx that are too big and rangy so as to be coarse-looking. Weak hind legs.

The Manx is one of the most interesting and unusual of all the cats. Lively, extremely brave, a patient and skillful hunter, and an affectionate companion, it is as famous for its rabbity hop as it is for its taillessness. Some people say the Manx is a cat-rabbit cross; this is nonsense—a biological impossibility.

Tailless cats are known in many parts of the world—Korea, Japan, southeast Asia, the South Sea islands, southern Russia, and so on. How these cats got to the Isle of Man—or whether they did—remains unknown, although legend says that a ship from the Spanish Armada which was wrecked on the island brought a tailless cat with it (there are no tailless cats in Spain, however). Manx men generally have believed that the tailless cat was brought to their island from the distant East long centuries ago.

Since the tailless cat is a mutant, there is no reason to believe that the Manx cat did not originate right on the Isle of Man. This genetic effect is incompletely dominant, which means that the mutation tends to perpetuate itself when bred with cats that do have tails.

This is fortunate, for a lethal factor is involved in the genetic makeup of the Manx. Breed tailless Manx to tailless Manx, and the third generation will produce feeble kittens. The kittens of the fourth generation will all be born dead.

But not all Manx are tailless, or "rumpies," as the islanders call them. In a Manx litter some may be tailless, some may have a stub of a tail (they're called "stumpies"), and some may even have complete tails.

Havana Brown (Chestnut)

HEAD: Should be longer than it is wide, with a distinct stop at the eyes. The head narrows to a fine muzzle with a slight break behind the whiskers. Allowance to be made for jowls in the stud cats.

WHISKERS: Must be brown.

EARS: Large, round-tipped, with very little hair inside or out; wide-set but not flaring.

EYES: The aperture should be oval. The color should be chartreuse to green, darker green shades preferred.

NECK: Must not be short.

BODY: Medium long, compact body. Hard and muscular.

LEGS AND FEET: Legs should be proportionately slender. Paws should be oval. Pads have rose tinge.

TAIL: Should be medium in length in proportion to the body.

COAT: Should be very glossy and sleek, but not as short as a Siamese coat.

COLOR: Any shade of rich, warm, mahogany brown. Entire cat to be the same shade of brown.

CONDITION: Hard and muscular. Coat must be glossy, eyes clear.

BALANCE: Straight body and legs. Well balanced physically and temperamentally. Gentle and amenable to handling.

UNDESIRABLE: Weak chin. Lack of stop. White whiskers. Siamese or Burmese type of body. Black pads. Thick or short tail. Dull, open or fluffy coat. White hairs in coat. Overweight or underweight.

This is the newest of all the breeds. It was first developed in Great Britain. The Havana Breeders Society, an American organization, says, "It is our understanding these [English] breeders set out to breed a solid brown cat comparable to the Swiss mountain cat." Havanas were first exhibited in the United States in 1959.

A quiet, clean, elegant cat, the Havana has a somewhat pixie-ish look about it that is very engaging. To the untutored eye, it looks a good deal like a Burmese—a mistake that draws frowns from the Havana Brown breeders.

Red Colorpoint Short-Hair

The standard for this breed is the same as for the Siamese, except that the color of the points should be a dense, deep red with all points of the same shade, and the body color should be clear white with shading, when present, in the same tone as the points.

This breed is new, very rare, and difficult to breed.

3. ACQUIRING A CAT

"... I have already selected a dirty little drunken wretch of a kitten to be successor to my poor old cat. I don't suppose it drinks anything stronger than milk and water but then, you know, so much milk and water must be bad for a kitten that age—at any rate it looks as if it drank; but it gives me the impression of being affectionate, intelligent, and fond of mice, and I believe if it had a home it would become more respectable; at any rate I will see how it works."

—SAMUEL BUTLER, in a letter to
Eliza Mary Anne Savage,
October 21, 1885

AMBROSE BIERCE defined the cat as "a soft, indestructible automaton provided by nature to be kicked when things go wrong in the domestic circle." If that is your idea of a cat, you shouldn't have one. On the other hand, if that were your philosophy, you wouldn't be reading this book, so it can safely be assumed that you do not agree with Bierce.

Not everyone should keep a cat. For example, it is not uncommon to hear a parent say the cat is wanted as a pet for the child. There's no harm in this— if the parents like cats and if they are prepared to take care of the cat. If they're getting the cat to teach the child a sense of responsibility by forcing the child to care for the cat, they are doing their child an injustice and committing an act of cruelty against the cat.

Cats require very little care, but they do require that minimum. If you are unprepared to give the cat that small part of your time and effort, you'd do better to get a stuffed doll or some other inanimate object to share your home with you. (A cat may also be inadvisable for a person who suffers from allergic disorders. This is quite uncommon—the *Encyclopaedia Britannica* says that only two to five per cent of the total population has allergies. But among those who do suffer from this nuisance, an allergy to cats is frequently found. This does not necessarily mean that the pleasure of a cat's company must be denied to such a person; it is possible to eliminate or diminish the allergy by desensitization. The author of this book, in fact, was found to be allergic to cats years ago, and he now enjoys an untroubled life with four of them!)

BABIES AND CATS

Just what kind of a home is it that this cat is going to enter? Is it a home with a baby in it?

If you do have a baby, don't worry about those old wives' tales of cats that suck the breath from infants. This is an absolutely untrue, unjustified libel on cats, but it is incredible how widespread it is—and among people who should know better, too. In 1941 a survey among young men in the camps of the Civilian Conservation Corps disclosed that thirty-four percent were certain that cats did suck babies' breath. And today people are still troubled by this fantasy; every year several readers of my newspaper column on pets write to me anxiously to say that they are about to have a baby and they're worried because they have a cat.

Dr. Morris Fishbein of the American Medical Association is authority for the statement that this is sheer superstition, undoubtedly spread by persons who are pathologically afraid of cats. And Professor Bergen Evans of Northwestern University, after investigating the matter, reported in his entertaining book, *The Natural History of Nonsense*, that "there is nothing to support the belief."

Of course, if you have a baby and a cat in the same household, it is only prudent not to leave the cat alone in the room where the baby is sleeping. Cats almost always love babies and children in general, sometimes too much. The cat is happiest when it can cuddle up to the baby in its crib. But if it does lie down in the crib with the baby, it may unintentionally harm the infant by lying on it.

If you have a baby, don't hesitate to get a cat. You'll make a baby and a cat happy.

On the other hand, if you have small children you must use considerable caution, for children, without meaning harm, can be too enthusiastic and too careless in their handling of small animals. Instead of a very young kitten, it's probably best to get a young cat—say, about six months old—if you have children under the age of seven or thereabouts. For it is a fallacy that cats always land on their feet; many cats suffer severe back injuries when they are dropped by children. A bigger cat can take care of itself more easily with children about than a little kitten can.

AND THEN THERE ARE DOGS

But suppose you have a dog? Can you then bring a cat into the house, too?

The answer to that lies in the temperament of the dog and your relations with it. Despite the old simile about "fighting like cats and dogs," cats and dogs can get along beautifully together in the house. If you have a dog that's extremely jealous, you'll probably have trouble bringing a cat into the house, although it can be done even under those circumstances, in most cases, if you lavish an unusual amount of affection and attention on the dog to make up for the intrusion. If the dog isn't jealous, it's unlikely you'll have any problem.

One word of caution, however: Let matters take their own course. Don't try to force the cat and the dog to make friends. These things take time. Stand ready to protect either animal in case of trouble, but leave them alone until trouble develops (it probably won't). In a few days, after they've investigated each other at a distance, they'll begin to relax. Give them a month or two, and you may find them sleeping together.

One of my own dogs—I breed Standard Schnauzers—was purchased as a full-grown bitch. She was a confirmed cat-hater, had even killed a couple of cats in the neighborhood where her previous owners lived. When she first arrived at my home, she was greeted at the door by four cats, who were delighted to see another dog. They loved their own dogs and assumed that all dogs loved cats as much as their dogs did.

The new dog's hackles went up, but she didn't try to attack the cats. Four of them were too formidable for that, especially in a strange new home. She decided to think things over for a few days. In a week or two she was cleaning cats from stem to stern every morning, playing with them, sleeping with them.

Not that she's given up hating cats, mind you. She still hates all cats but her own. On a summer day, she and her canine mate will stand on the screened-in porch, barking deadly threats at a cat across the street, while her own four cats sit beside her, apparently cheering her on.

WHAT KIND OF CAT?

With any such difficulties out of the way, we can assume that you do want a cat. Now you must decide what kind: Pedigreed or plain old alley? Long-hair or short-hair? Male or female? Kitten or cat?

Between the pedigreed cat and the ordinary puss of uncertain ancestry there is not as much difference as one might suppose. You can be sure that either will give you affection, amusement, companionship, esthetic pleasure, and all the other innumerable benefits of life with a cat. I have both, and I'd hate to have to choose between them.

It's true, of course, that with an ordinary cat you're buying a pig in a poke. You don't know anything about the cat's ancestry. Its color, structure, size, and temperament will all be matters for speculation until it grows up.

This doesn't really matter terribly, as all of us who have had the privilege of sharing our lives with ordinary—as though *any* cat were ever ordinary!—cats can attest.

GETTING A CAT

How are you going to get this cat?
There are any number of different ways.

You may open the door one day and there it will be, on your doorstep, just waiting for you. In a crowd of people, a cat may walk past a half dozen people to rub against your legs and claim you as its own. A friend's cat may have kittens—helpless little things, all in need of homes. You may be accosted one day by a neighbor's child who holds his cat up to you and says, "My mother won't let me keep it."

If it doesn't just happen, like that—a cat's adopting you, in a manner of speaking—you'll have to go looking for a cat. Many pet shops have unregistered cats at very low prices, usually between two and ten dollars; many pet shops give such kittens away free, on the assumption that anyone who gives a kitten a home will be a future customer for cat supplies.

Another place to get a cat is your local animal shelter. Taking a cat from an animal shelter can give you the extra satisfaction of knowing that you have saved one cat from the terrible mass slaughter that takes place every day. In New York City alone, nearly *one hundred thousand* cats must be destroyed every year; that's over 270 cats a day! Animal shelters are only too happy to give away cats free in order to cut down this ghastly toll.

THE PEDIGREED CAT

If it's a pedigreed cat that you want, you'll have to take a little more care about finding a cat.

Your first problem is selecting the right breed. There is a breed, as Chapter 2 indicates, for every conceivable taste—a long-hair for elegance, a Siamese for playfulness, blues for handsomeness, and so on. But if you choose a long-hair, you must ask yourself whether you are prepared to give it the painstaking daily care that a long-hair requires.

You must be prepared to pay a fair price for a pedigreed cat. The price is likely to be a little higher than you expected to pay. But the price will have to cover all the breeder's costs, including purchase and care of the queen, perhaps a stud fee, care of the queen in pregnancy, veterinary fees, care of the kittens after birth, inoculations, etc. The costs of breeding good animals are much greater than most people suppose. Breeding cats is a hobby and the people who enjoy it are lucky if they break even on costs. Nobody's making a profit.

If you want to get an idea of how prices are, drop into a pet shop and buy a copy of *All-Pets Magazine*. This monthly magazine carries a regular feature entitled "Petstock Market Report," which lists the prices that various pet animals have been selling at on the retail market throughout the country. As these words are written, for example, *All-Pets* says that Siamese cats have been selling between a low of ten dollars and a high of forty-five dollars, and Persians, a low of twenty and a high of fifty.

Those are pet-shop prices. Breeders themselves will charge fifty to one hundred percent more than pet-shop prices generally. This is not, as you might incorrectly guess, an attempt by the breeders to charge all the traffic will bear. The breeders charge more because their cats are better than pet-shop cats.

This should be obvious. After all, the pet-shop cats themselves were purchased from the breeders in the first place. If they were as good as the breeders wanted them to be, the breeders would have kept them and sold them themselves. Instead, they sold them for next to nothing to a pet shop. (It can be assumed that the pet shop paid the breeder less than half the price that the pet shop charges for the kittens. That's the usual markup.)

The breeders keep the strongest, healthiest cats, the best specimens of their breed, to be sold at their own catteries. If you want to buy these cats—the finest, both show quality and pet quality—you must deal with the breeders. But how are you to locate them?

Many of the best breeders advertise at least once a week in the local newspapers, usually on the day when the newspaper's pet column or cat column—if it carries such features—appears.

Another way to find cat breeders is to attend a cat show in your area. About one hundred and twenty such shows are held throughout the country every year. This means that at least one or two cat shows will be held in your city, or within a short automobile trip of it, in a year's time. These shows often are announced in the newspapers. They are also listed, months in advance, in *Cats Magazine*.

If you buy a pedigreed cat, there are two precautions that you must take:

1. Make sure that the breeder (or pet-shop dealer) explicitly agrees that the cat can be returned within a given period—say, forty-eight or seventy-two hours—if it does not pass a veterinarian's examination for health and soundness.

2. Make sure that the cat's "papers" are transferred to you at the time you pay for the cat. This is the registration certificate that attests to the fact that the cat's records, including its pedigree, have been kept by one or more of the six stud-book organizations: the American Cat Association, the American Cat Fanciers' Association, the Cat Fanciers' Association, the Cat Fanciers' Federation, the National Cat Fanciers' Association, and the United Cat Federation.

MALE OR FEMALE?

Now, whether you're getting a pedigreed cat or an unregistered pet, you are at the point where you must make another decision: Should you get a male or a female?

If all you want is a pet, it doesn't matter which you get. There is no substantial difference between males and females in temperament or any other important quality. Both should be neutered before they're a year old. This question is discussed at greater length in Chapter 9.

If, however, you want to breed and exhibit cats, then you ought to buy a female, not a male. The chances are that you'll want to keep your cat in your home, and an adult male simply cannot be kept in the house unless it is castrated; the odor is not to be endured. A female, on the other hand, will prove difficult only when she is in heat.

This is as good a time as any to tell you how to distinguish between a male and a female cat. It's not as easy as you might think. The sex of a cat, unlike that of a dog, cow, or almost any other animal you can think of, is not readily identifiable. You must lift the cat's tail to find out. A male kitten's undeveloped sex organs look like a punctuation mark, the colon(:). The female's look like an inverted exclamation mark (ı).

ACQUIRING A CAT

KITTEN OR CAT?

The next decision that you must make involves the age of the cat. Do you want a little kitten or should you get a grown cat instead?

This question, of course, will not concern you if you've adopted—or been adopted by—a stray. But you may wonder about it if you're setting out deliberately to procure a cat.

Generally, you'll be better off with a kitten. An adult has already formed its own habits and its way of life. There may be some adjustment difficulties until you and the cat agree upon a *modus vivendi*, especially if the cat was used to living with somebody else. But don't let this discourage you. Much depends on how you and the cat hit it off. If you take to each other, there won't be any problems at all. I've known many people who took home adult cats and had a wonderful life with them from the first day.

A kitten, of course, is at a more malleable stage of life. It will grow up with the habits that you let it acquire. It will adjust itself to your way of life.

Generally, it is best to choose a kitten that is nine or ten weeks old, because by then the kitten is big enough and strong enough to survive without its mother. You'd better not take a younger kitten unless you're the kind of person who can take care of any animal without any trouble. If the kitten is very young, you will have to be a substitute mother for it, and there are a lot of unexpected jobs to do if you intend to fill that role. (See Chapter 6.) Of course, the age of your children can be a factor, too, in your choice of a cat, as the discussion earlier in this chapter pointed out.

WHAT TO LOOK FOR

Now you're at the point of picking a cat. This is a moment when you must really be on your toes.

If you're buying your cat from a breeder, his reputation stands behind the kitten, so you've got a certain amount of insurance against error. But 999 out of every 1,000 cats—that's a statistic that I just made up—come from the litters of friends' cats, animal shelters, or other miscellaneous sources, and nothing will protect you from an unhappy mistake in that case except the fine old rule of *caveat emptor* —"let the buyer beware."

Take a look at the litter as a whole before you begin looking at individual kittens. Let's say there are six kittens. Five of them are playing with the mock-ferocity of young tigers. One sits sadly in the corner, looking shy and lonely. Your heart goes out to it—this kitten obviously needs a home and comforting. But don't give in to the impulse. The kitten may be shy, but it's more likely that it's staying out of things because it's sick. The lively, saucy, friendly kitten is usually the safer choice.

Now it's time to begin looking at each kitten. Check each one for health and then for soundness.

If there are bare spots anywhere in the coat, the kitten may have ringworm. Beware of scales on the eyelids or running eyes. Look into the ears; if they don't look clean, the kitten may have mites. The nose should not be running, although it can be wet and cold, of course. Lift up the tail and look carefully around the vent for any signs of diarrhea; the fur of the back legs may also give a clue to this.

Now consider the cat's condition. Does it weigh as much and is it as big as you would expect a kitten to be at that age? (Remember that a Siamese, say, is not going to weigh as much as a long-hair at the same age.) Shake some keys in the air behind the kitten and see if it whips its head around; that's one rough test of the cat's hearing. See if the kitten blinks its eyes when its light is cut off suddenly.

SEEING A VETERINARIAN

These precautions are enough when you're getting the kitten. But you'd better take it immediately to a veterinarian (see Chapter 6 on choosing a vet). He can detect trouble signs that you'd never notice. I say *immediately* because the longer you have the kitten, the harder it will be for you to return it, no matter how sick or malformed it may be. Tell the veterinarian that you have just obtained the cat and you want a thorough examination of it for health and soundness.

ACQUIRING A CAT

While you've got the kitten at the veterinarian's office, ask the doctor to give it the first of its immunization shots against distemper and pneumonitis.

The veterinarian is also the person with whom to discuss any special problems the kitten may have with regard to feeding or general care, subjects that will be discussed in later chapters.

ASK QUESTIONS

Before you take the kitten from the person who had it, talk to him at some length about the manner in which the kitten has been cared for up to now. This is of particular importance if you have not been used to caring for young animals. You can use all the information, advice, and help you can get.

Find out—and write down, for you'll forget it otherwise—what the kitten is accustomed to eating, and at what times. Be sure that the information includes quantities, too.

Has the kitten been housebroken in its toilet habits? If it has been, was it trained to go outdoors or in a sanitary pan in the house?

All these things are important, because you cannot change a kitten's way of doing things overnight without upsetting it terribly. In the beginning, you should imitate as closely as possible the care it has been receiving, and gradually, over the next few days, begin changing those things which seem to require change.

CARRYING THE CAT

It's unlikely that you'll have a carrying case when you go to pick up your cat, so you'd better take a big, thick, bath towel with you. That's to wrap around the cat.

The towel serves two purposes: it protects you and it comforts the cat. You may need protection because the cat is likely to be frightened, and frightened cats tend to claw frantically. After all, the cat has never seen you before. All it knows is that a stranger has picked it up and is taking it, perhaps in a car, through a bewildering, strange new area of unfamiliar sights and sounds and smells. But the cat can't claw you in its panic if you've wrapped it well in the towel and keep a firm grip on it. Unable to escape, the cat will then want to hide from the fearsome world. Cats love to hide their faces under those circumstances. The towel offers it that hiding place.

As soon as possible, however, you should buy a carrying case. Every pet shop carries cat cases. Some are made of basketweave, others are solid-sided boxes with air holes at each end and a handle at the top. A carrying case is invaluable when you have to take a cat to the veterinarian, or to a boarding kennel, or on a trip.

EQUIPMENT

The carrying case is not the only equipment you'll need. Let's see what else there is.

House training will be discussed in the next section. The equipment you'll need for this will be a sanitary pan of plastic, aluminum, or enamel-coated metal; a bag of litter to put in the pan; and a little sieve-shovel for sifting the solid matter out of the pan every day. All these articles are available in your pet shop.

Although most cats will pick their own beds, you'll probably want to provide one at the start. If the new cat is a kitten, a bed is essential. You can buy one at the pet shop or fix your own. A box makes an excellent bed (especially if you can cover half the box so the cat can feel that it is sleeping in a cave). The bed, by the way, should not be placed on the floor, but on a chest or trunk, so that it will be out of the way of drafts. How long the cat sleeps in its bed depends on you. If you permit it, the cat's almost certain to share your bed with you after it settles down in your house.

The bedding should help the cat conserve its body heat. The best bed is newspaper with a blanket laid on top of it. The blanket should not be neat and flat, but pushed roughly into the bed box, so that the cat can wriggle around and get the blanket up around itself. The blanket will need frequent laundering, of course, and if the cat has gotten itself wet, you can assume the blanket will get wet, too. Don't let the cat sleep on a wet blanket.

A brush and a comb for grooming the cat are also necessities. The kind of brush will depend to some extent on the hair-length of the coat. The bristles should be firm, but not set so close together that they cannot get down through the fur. Some all-plastic pet brushes are available now, and they are just right for your purpose. The comb is used for working mats out of the hair, so a relatively open-toothed comb, which your pet shop carries, is indicated.

Nail clippers are essential. The kind of clippers used for human fingernails are perfect.

A collar is indicated, preferably with an identification tag attached to it giving your name, address, and telephone number. Innumerable cats are strangled to death by their collars, so you'd better be careful about the kind of collar you buy. It should be one that will expand and release the cat if the collar gets caught on a nail or the limb of a tree. One excellent safety collar has one side of elastic material that will stretch to let the cat escape if it gets caught.

If you live in the city or the suburbs, and you want to take the cat outdoors—and you should do that from time to time in good weather— you'll need a round leather collar and a leash to fasten to it. Light leashes especially made for cats can be found in pet shops. You may also want to buy one of the special harnesses made for walking cats; they are better than a collar for this purpose.

HOUSEBREAKING

Nothing could be easier than training a cat—even a kitten—to use a sanitary pan. Cats are naturally clean animals. Three and a half centuries ago Edward Topsell, the first English zoologist, said of the cat, "Her nature is to hide her own dung or excrement, for she knoweth that the favor and presence thereof will drive away her sport, the little mouse being able by that stool to smell the presence of her mortal foe." Whether that is the reason why the cat buries its waste no one knows, but certainly the cat's instinct makes it loath to do its business where it cannot bury it.

The sanitary pan—or "cat box," as most cat owners call it—should be put in one place and kept there. Under the sink in the bathroom is one of the most convenient places for most households. The cat should be taken to the box, which has been filled with clean litter. Put the cat in the box so it can tell that this is a place where unpleasant things can be buried. If you have a kitten, take its forepaws in your hands and gently dig a hole in the litter with them, to give the kitten the idea.

Then keep your eye on the cat. You'll be able to guess when it needs to use the box; the look of discomfort and uneasiness is usually quite clear. When the cat looks as though it might need the box, take it there again.

You must expect one or two mistakes on the part of the cat. As soon as you find such a mishap, hold the cat close to it—do *not* touch its nose to it!—and give it a light slap while scolding it. Then take it to the box and keep it there for a few moments.

Some cats are easier to train than others. I have never had a cat that made more than two mistakes before learning what the box was for. On the other hand, I have brought into my home kittens that were only six weeks old and never made a single mistake.

Once the cat is housebroken, you need not worry about its hygienic habits except for two things.

The first is a fireplace. Unfortunately, the ashes in a fireplace strike many cats as an excellent place to hide their dirt. From a cat's point of view, there is a certain logic to this. But it can be an unpleasant practice from the owner's point of view. The best way to handle this problem is to punish the cat, but also to keep the fireplace as clear of ashes as possible when no fire is lit. It may also help to put a fireplace screen before the fire pit so that the cat just can't get in.

The second problem may puzzle you. Your cat, let us say, is and has been housebroken perfectly. You've been able to trust it for months. Suddenly it begins to disgrace itself. This sort of thing can be quite a shock to the complacent cat owner.

There can be two explanations. One is that the cat is suffering from cystitis (see Chapter 7), in which case you'd better take it to the veterinarian for treatment.

But before you go running off to the veterinarian, investigate the second possibility—that you yourself are at fault!

You can be at fault if you've neglected to take proper care of the cat box. If the litter needs changing or sifting, the cat may refuse to use it. If the need continues, and you do nothing about it, the cat may take the law into its own hands and demonstrate forcefully to you its desire for a clean box.

The cat box should be sifted once a day. The litter should be changed as often as necessary. No set time can be stated, for the condition of the litter is affected by many factors: the kind of litter that is used, the number of cats using the box, and the kind of weather you've been having. No one litter seems best for all cats; some litters will cover the odor of one cat best, others will be better for covering the odor of another cat. The weather comes into play because several rainy days, during which the litter never dries, will make the cat box objectionable.

One last word about this matter of housebreaking: Some people train their cats to use a toilet. It's a nice trick, and convenient, if you want to take the trouble.

It takes about a month to train a cat to use the toilet. You must begin with a cat that is trained to use a sanitary pan. Encourage the cat to jump up on the seat by putting the pan there. But you must secure the pan so it won't slip when she jumps in or out. Cut a slit two inches wide down the length of the pan, in the middle. Put litter around the side of the slit or fashion a stall which will force the cat to poise itself over the slit. When it is used to doing its business under those circumstances, take the pan away and substitute a platform, with a two-inch slit down the middle of it, for the pan. Eventually, if you wish, you can remove the platform and the cat will continue to use the toilet, balancing itself on the sides of the seat.

THE ESSENTIAL REQUIREMENT

By now it must seem to you that a cat is a great deal of trouble. It isn't.

In practice, preparing for a cat is as simple as it sounds complex. It is much easier, for example, than bringing a dog into your home. As a dog breeder, I know—I've had to adjust to both animals.

If I have given the impression that the cat needs to be treated like a delicate flower, I've misled you. It is extremely hardy, ingenious, and resilient. But all cats have intricate psychological and physiological systems. And kittens have the special vulnerability of all young life.

Try to put yourself in the cat's, or the kitten's, place. You are wrenched from the place that has been familiar to you, carried by a strange human in a strange vehicle through strange streets to a strange new house. It can be a shattering experience.

The cat needs not only care, but love and understanding, too. A soothing tone of voice, the stroke of a comforting hand on a furry little head, a warm lap to lie on—these are the things that can ease the strain on a cat during its first few days in your home.

Don't try to grab the cat, or make sudden moves toward it. You'll only frighten the little thing. Don't use a loud voice or permit loud noises until the cat is settled down with you and you've adjusted to each other.

If you have children, keep them away from the cat for a day or two. If you have a dog or another cat, don't try to force them to make friends with the newcomer; you'll just get everyone upset and annoyed.

But if you use patience, understanding, care, and love, your cat will very quickly be a part of the household. Then you will know what Mark Twain meant when he wrote, "A house without a cat, and a well-fed, well-petted, and properly revered cat, may be a perfect house, perhaps, but how can it prove its title?"

4. THE NATURE OF
THE CAT

When my cat and I entertain each other with mutual apish tricks, as playing with a garter, who knows but that I make my cat more sport than she makes me? Shall I conclude her to be simple, that has her time to begin or refuse to play as freely as I myself have? Nay, who knows but that it is a defect of my not understanding her language (for doubtless cats talk and reason with one another) that we agree no better? And who knows but that she pities me for being no wiser than to play with her, and laughs and censures my folly for making sport for her, when we two play together?

MICHEL DE MONTAIGNE (1533-1592)

CATS and people have a good deal more in common than their mutual preferences for warmth, dry places, good food, and soft beds. Cats have too much in common with people for their own good, in fact, for the similarities are so marked that the cat is considered one of the best substitutes for man in experiments. (This use of the cat, happily, is limited by the intractable character of the cat when it is subjected to something it doesn't like.)

Think of the cat's body as you think of your own, and you won't be terribly far off the mark. Both are mammals. Both have a four-chambered heart and the same circulatory systems to carry the blood on its circuit through the body. Both have noses, windpipes, and paired lungs for breathing. Both have the same internal organs: stomach, pancreas, liver, kidneys, small intestine, large intestine. Each has a brain and a central nervous system. The bone structures of both are quite similar; run down the names of the cat's bones and see how familiar they sound—occiput, cranium, vertebrae, ribs, sacrum, ilium, fibula, tibia, tarsus, metatarsus, humerus, radius, ulna, carpus, metacarpus, and so on.

It should be obvious that there are marked differences between the body of a man and the body of a cat, despite the similarities. Have you tried touching your tongue to your back lately?

There are more important differences, of course. The tolerance of a cat to drugs is not at all that of a human. The cat can contract feline distemper, to which you are immune (and so is your dog, by the way, for this is different from canine distemper); you can get the mumps, but the cat can't. All of this, one must add hastily, is stated on the basis of present knowledge.

In Chapter 8 we'll go into the question of disease more fully, but at this point it might be illuminating to run down a list of some of the ills to which the cat is a prey and see how many are familiar names of human maladies: anemia, bronchitis, cancer, cirrhosis of the liver, dandruff, diabetes, eczema, encephalitis, food poisoning, heart disease, hernia, jaundice, obesity, pleurisy, ringworm, shock, tooth decay, uremia, virus infections.

Nevertheless, the cat is a different creature from man—and from dog, too. Zoologists consider the dog, in Dr. Edwin H. Colbert's words, "structurally primitive," in contrast with the cat, which is "highly evolved."

A knowledge of this sophisticated organism, with its peculiarities, may help you better to enjoy life with your cat. So let us see what kind of a creature this *Felis catus* is.

SKIN AND HAIR

The hair that has almost vanished from most of man's body still covers the cat thickly. All cats have fur, even the so-called "hairless" cat of Mexico, New Mexico, and Uruguay, which has a fine, almost imperceptible covering. The fur grows everywhere on the cat's body except for three places: the nose, the pads of the feet, the anus, and the nipples.

It is worth considering, for a moment, how the hair grows and how the skin nurtures it. The skin, as in man, consists of two layers, the outer, called the *epidermis,* and the inner, the *dermis.* The epidermis, also known as the cuticle or scarfskin, is made up in turn of four layers. The deepest of these is the level at which regeneration takes place—where new skin is produced constantly.

The skin is not an absolute barrier, even when it is unpunctured. Although it is waterproof, it does permit the absorption of some oils and drugs. This is an important point to remember: I have seen a kitten paralyzed—only temporarily, fortunately—by chemical baths it was given to cure a purely external skin condition. The drug had been absorbed through the skin, and its effect was toxic.

The hair grows out of follicles, or sacs, which are buried in the skin. Attached to the follicles are tiny erector muscles. You have a few such muscles yourself at the back of your neck; that's why you can "feel your hair stand on end" when you're frightened. The cat's body is covered with such muscles. When it is frightened or angry, it seems as though almost every hair on its body stands erect. Even the fur on the tail stands out so that it looks as though the slim tail has suddenly been turned into a fox's full brush. It has been theorized that this phenomenon is a gift of nature to the cat in the form of a psychological weapon with which to frighten its enemies. With all its fur fluffed up and its back arched, a small cat, spitting and growling, can look like a most formidable foe.

The skin also contains the sweat glands. There are sweat glands in the pads of the cat's feet, but it's doubtful how much these glands have to do with regulating the temperature of the body. These, and the sweat glands in the skin, do help in the elimination of impurities, however.

More common than the sweat glands are the sebaceous glands of the skin. Most of these glands open into the hair follicles. Their secretion, a substance called *sebum,* an oily, semiliquid material which solidifies when it is exposed to hair, coats the hair as it grows up through and out of the skin. Around the follicles are also other cells, called *melanoblasts,* which are believed to produce melanins, the substances of which pigment is composed. Granules of pigment are deposited in the follicles as the hair grows, and the color of the coat reflects the activities of these cells in the skin.

One of the most remarkable qualities of the cat's skin is its speed in regeneration and its ability, as the cat's first line of resistance, to fight off infection when it is invaded as a result of a wound.

SKELETON

Man may be roughly fifteen times the size of the cat, but he has fewer bones. To be precise, the cat has 230 bones in its skeleton, while man has only 206. Their distribution is different, too.

The cat has thirteen ribs; man has twelve. Both have seven cervical vertebrae. The cat has thirteen thoracic vertebrae, one more than man, and seven lumbar vertebrae, two more than man. But man has five sacral vertebrae, compared with the cat's three. When it comes to the coccygeal vertebrae—the tail—there is, as you might suppose, a considerable difference between cat and man. Man usually has four or five of these vestigial tailbones, while the cat's tailbones can range from none (in the Manx) to twenty-eight; most cats have between eighteen and twenty-three.

Nevertheless, if you stood the skeleton of a cat on its back legs so that it was erect, like a man, you'd find almost a bone-for-bone identity with man. Many of the bones have been modified in the cat to adapt to its special needs, but they are still essentially the same bones.

The modifications, however, can cause important distinctions between cat and man. To get back to the question that arose earlier, why *can't* you touch your tongue to your back like a cat, always assuming, of course, that you wanted to do it?

There are two basic reasons for the cat's incredible flexibility of body. The first reason is its shoulder joint, which is free and relatively open, permitting the cat to turn its foreleg in almost any direction without undue strain. The second reason is the clavicle (collarbone) —or the lack of it. In cats this bone is very small in comparison with man's; many cats have no clavicle at all.

All these bones are manipulated by more than five hundred voluntary skeletal muscles, which can twist the cat into some amazing shapes when it so desires. One of the few useful physiological features which the cat does not possess—and man does—is the thumb. You can feel the cat's equivalent of the thumb on the inside of the leg about the point where it meets the foot. The claw is there, but the bone that would be the thumb has never properly developed.

The feet and claws of a cat deserve some attention. One notable fact is that the cat walks on its toes. That part of the foot which includes the palm, instep, heel, and ankle in man forms the lowest part of the leg in the cat.

Polydactylism—extra toes—is frequently encountered in the cat, because it is a hereditary trait carried by a dominant gene. Usually it takes the form of six toes on each front foot, but sometimes the cat will have seven toes on the front feet, six on the hind feet.

The claws are, as everyone who has ever played with a cat knows full well, rectractile; that is, the cat can withdraw them into their sheaths or slip them out at will. Usually the claws are sheathed when the cat walks, unless it is on a slippery surface.

There is still another unusual aspect of the cat's skeleton and moving structure. The cat does not run like the dog or the horse or most other animals. When those other animals walk or run, the left front leg moves when the right hind leg moves, and the right front leg moves when the left hind leg moves. Not so the cat. It moves the front and back legs on one side, then the front and back legs on the other side. Only two other animals move like this—the camel and the giraffe.

NERVOUS SYSTEM

The brain and central nervous system of the cat are very much like the dog's, but somewhat different from man's. In all three, the brain is divided into the cerebrum, the front part, and the cerebellum, the lower part.

The cerebrum, which is the seat of conscious, deliberate, rational actions, is smaller in the cat and the dog than in man. This does not mean that the cat is not intelligent—on the contrary, it is a highly rational creature.

The cerebellum, which is the seat of instinct, unconscious memory, and reflex actions, is as highly developed in cats as in dogs. Scratch your cat on its back just in front of its tail, and it will automatically arch its tail and lift its hindquarters; this involuntary action is directed by the cerebellum. Many veterinarians, when they are anesthetizing a cat, will test the level of the cat's consciousness and its sensitivity by tugging gently on the hair that grows between the pads on the bottom of the foot. If the cat pulls up its foot instantly in a reflex action, the cerebellum is still functioning and deep anesthesia has not yet been achieved.

The cat's nervous system is designed to make it one of the most alert and perceptive animals on earth. For example, the *vibrissae*, the stiff whiskers growing out from the sides of the muzzle, are sensory organs. They have very acute nerves at their root, which transmit messages to the brain. Thus the cat, blindfolded in tests, can put his front feet firmly on a table if only his whiskers have touched its edge. The whiskers are important to the cat in getting about at night, as we shall see (below) when we begin considering the cat's eyes.

DIGESTIVE SYSTEM

The cat's organs of digestion are very much the same as man's: mouth, esophagus, stomach, duodenum, small intestine, large intestine, rectum. The processes that take place in those organs differ a good deal from the activities that take place in the human digestive system.

The difference begins in the mouth. This is where digestion begins, but it is far more important to man than to the cat, for food remains in the man's mouth longer. A cat, on the contrary, tears off a piece of meat, chews it very briefly, and swallows it. The salivary juices have little time to work on it. But they do have some time.

However, the salivary juices in a cat's mouth are not the same as in man's. The biggest difference concerns an enzyme called *ptyalin*, which helps to break down starches into blood sugar. There is a good deal of ptyalin in the human mouth, but scarcely any in the cat's. This means that starches are relatively untouched by the digestive process in the cat until they reach the small intestine—and food doesn't remain there very long.

The stomach juices in the cat are a great deal stronger than in a human stomach. They are so strong, in fact, that in an hour they can break down hard bone to a soft, pliable state like cartilage. This does not mean that it's all right to feed bones to your cat. It isn't.

The cat's stomach is surprisingly sensitive, which is good for the cat. If a cat eats a mouse, it will retain the nutritive parts of the rodent and regurgitate the hair, bones, and nails. It will also regurgitate most foods that it has difficulty digesting.

One curse of man's digestive tract also bedevils the cat—ulcers. The cat can, and not infrequently does, develop ulcers in the stomach, duodenum, or small intestine—which may be considered another proof of what an intelligent, highly developed animal it is.

MOUTH AND TEETH

The cat has thirty teeth as an adult, which means that the human is two teeth to the good. The teeth bear the same names as those bestowed on human teeth: incisors (the shearing teeth at the front), canines (the fangs), premolars, and molars.

The kitten's full set of teeth look like this:

UPPER JAW: six incisors, two canines, six molars.

LOWER JAW: six incisors, two canines, four molars.

The adult cat's full set is arranged thusly:

UPPER JAW: six incisors, two canines, six premolars, two molars.

LOWER JAW: six incisors, two canines, four premolars, two molars.

The teething process in kittens, and problems attendant on it, are discussed in Chapter 6. Dental problems in the adult cat are dealt with in Chapter 7.

Cleft lips and cleft palates occur occasionally in cats. Sometimes surgery can remedy the condition, but it is usually better to let the kitten be put to sleep.

Lacking the sphincter muscle of the mouth which the human possesses, the cat can use its lips only to keep food and liquids in its mouth. Fortunately for us, it can't make faces with its lips.

The tongue's upper surface is a rasping tool. It is covered with minute hooks of four different shapes. With this rough tongue, the cat is admirably equipped to lick every last trace of meat off a bone and to brush its coat spotlessly clean. (Thanks to its flexible body, as we have seen, the cat can reach with its tongue all of its body except the back of the neck and the small area between the shoulder blades.)

The tongue is also used as a spoon with which to lap up liquids.

As the owners of some cats know, the tongue may also be used to express affection. One of the cats that shares my home with me "kisses" with his rough little tongue very frequently, purring brokenly all the while.

EYES, EARS, AND NOSE

The eyes of the cat are so spectacular that they have lent themselves to gems, folklore, and demonology.

Superficially the eyes are very much like man's. There are a couple of minor differences, however. One is the mictitating membrane, the "third eyelid," in the lower part of the eye. This helps to protect the eye. It is also a diagnostic aid to the veterinarian, for it sometimes will partly cover the iris if the cat is suffering from an intestinal disorder. (Nobody knows why.)

Another obvious difference is the iridescent layer of cells, called the *tapetum lucidum,* on the retina. These cells reflect light, which is why a cat's eyes shine at night.

The eyes not uncommonly are unmatched in color. But what the cat sees through those eyes—regardless of whether both are blue, or green, or whether each eye is a different color—is gray, or so most scientists believe. It is theorized that cats are color-blind, and that they are sensitive only to the intensity of a shade. Although some cats appear to prefer objects of a particular color, they do so for other, less obvious reasons, according to present speculation—because of the way the object smells, or its shape, for example.

One of the hardiest of myths about the cat is the belief that it can see in the dark. If by "dark" we mean total darkness, there is no truth to this. It is true, however, that the cat does see much better at night than man does. After all, the cat is basically a nocturnal animal. Visual purple in the epithelial rods of the retina is said to be the reason for the cat's excellent night vision. The cat can even see ultraviolet rays and other light invisible to us.

To compensate for its night vision, perhaps, the cat has been denied day vision on a par with ours. It sees better at dusk than at noon on a bright, sunny day. The ability of the cat's pupil to contract and expand in order to accomodate the amount of light available explains why the eye looks different every time we see it. In darkness, the pupil is at its widest to admit every possible bit of illumination. In bright sunlight, it is narrowed to a thin slit to cut down on the light pouring into the eye. It is an old folk belief, all over the world, that one can tell the time of day by the shape of the cat's pupil. You can test this yourself and see the falsity of it.

The ear of the cat is extremely sensitive to sound. Cats can distinguish even between the sounds of several motors of the same make, if one of them is in a car belonging to the cat's owner. Like dogs, cats can hear many sounds that are inaudible to the human ear. Research has indicated that the cat may be able to hear sounds that are even beyond the range of a dog's ear. The dog's range is believed to be close to twenty-five thousand cycles a second, compared with fifteen thousand for the human.

Like many breeds of dog, the cat has a naturally erect ear that helps to catch sound in the same way that a parabola microphone does.

Inside the cat's ear, however, is something quite different from the interior of the dog's ear. What that difference is, nobody has yet been able to discover. But we know it exists. For the cat—unlike man and the dog—is highly resistant to motion sickness. And motion sickness is intimately associated with the sense of balance; this, in turn, is dependent on the membranous labyrinth found in the internal ear. When the labyrinth is removed surgically from both ears, a dog is no longer liable to motion sickness.

Why is the cat virtually immune to motion sickness—that is, car sickness or seasickness—although it has the labyrinth intact? At this moment, no one knows.

The nose, cold and moist in a healthy cat (unless the cat has been sleeping), is the smallest part of the cat's olfactory system. The internal organs of scent are much larger than one might expect of such a small animal. The size of those organs, in fact, tells us that the cat, myths to the contrary, has a very keen sense of smell. All the other animals with sensitive noses have large internal scent organs.

From a considerable distance a cat can distinguish—by scent—the sex of another cat. This causes of good deal of confusion when a whole cat catches the scent of a neutered cat. It just doesn't smell right. This may explain why neutered and whole cats almost inevitably get into fights when they are loose and encounter each other.

Most of the odors we dislike the cat dislikes, too, for he is not a carrion eater, as the dog is. On the other hand, cats are very fond of perfume, hand lotion, and eau de Cologne. One of my own cats appears to become slightly intoxicated by such a fragrance.

The delight of cats with catnip is well known. If you grow catnip in your backyard, you can expect to have the neighborhood cats visiting you often. Diluted oil of catnip has been used with considerable success as a lure of bobcats and pumas. A small glass jar with the solution in it, capped by a perforated lid, will still draw the wild cats six to ten months after it has been buried in the ground with only the cap exposed, according to Stanley P. Young of the Fish and Wildlife Service of the United States Department of the Interior.

How the catnip affects the cat internally is still a matter of conjecture. But give the cat a few leaves of catnip, and it will behave in a weird and wonderful fashion—purring, growling, rolling on its back, play-fighting, rubbing itself against the mint, and carrying on generally in what can only be described as an orgiastic manner. It is almost certain that catnip—or cat mint, as it is also called—excites the cat sexually. It is also believed to have a soothing effect on its nervous system. (Those two effects of catnip might seem to be contradictory, but that's what the scientists say.)

There are other scents pleasing to the cat. Among them are valerian, lavender, violet, patchouli, wallflower, bean, some roses, and silver vine.

THE NATURE OF THE CAT

THE VOICE

No animal on earth is as capable of expressing itself as the cat. The basic element in its voice is the vocal cords. These are the superior (false) vocal cords and the inferior (true) vocal cords.

The way in which the cords are used by the cat is still not understood. It has been theorized that the cat's various calls are produced by the true vocal cords and its purrs by the false vocal cords. Why no other animal purrs is also a mystery.

There are many different purring sounds that every cat can make. One purr means contentment, affection. Another purr, harsher and deeper, means pain. There are many messages in purrs.

All cats purr, although the purring of some is inaudible. However, even with those cats one can feel the vibration by touching the cat's throat. Sometimes a cat that has been purring audibly becomes silent and, conversely, a cat that has been purring inaudibly suddenly begins to fill the room with sound.

Kittens begin to purr when they are about a week old. From then on they're likely to purr whenever they want to express their state of mind. Some cats will even purr when they are in a light sleep.

The ultimate expression of happiness on the part of many cats is to purr deeply and drool a few drops of saliva at the same time.

Young cats purr in a monotone, but older cats usually purr on two and sometimes even three notes.

The cat's calls are more varied than its purrs. Many persons have found, upon study, that the cat has more than thirty different calls, and some have counted as many as one hundred. There is the meow of greeting to the humans, a different meow of hunger, a welcome meow that sounds like a chirp, a meow of threat to another cat, and so on.

The growls are almost as varied. And there are spitting sounds, hisses, and screams. There is the caterwauling of the mating time and the caterwauling that is simply a serenade to the moon.

The cat even has physical means of expressing its feelings. Its tail is the most eloquent. Gently waving, it tells of the cat's quiet pleasure. Whipping from side to side, it expresses annoyance. Held out stiffly behind, the threat of imminent attack. Held vertically in the air—with possibly a crook at the very tip—a benign sense that all's well with the world.

The paws are often used to express love. This is the meaning of the "kneading" action that sometimes puzzles new cat owners. The cat stands on its owner's lap or even on a bed or a pile of clothes and works its fore paws with great determination, as though it were kneading bread dough. It looks a little as though the cat were playing an imaginary piano. This is an infallible sign that the cat is happy and bursting with affection. I believe that the action is a carry over from infancy, for the kitten, when nursing, employs the same kneading motion on both sides of the teat.

Each cat has its own language. One must listen to its voice, and watch its expressive tail, to interpret what it is saying.

INTELLIGENCE

Webster's New World Dictionary defines "intelligence" in these terms:

1. "The ability to learn or understand from experience; ability to acquire and retain knowledge; mental ability."

2. "The ability to respond quickly and successfully to a new situation; use of the faculty of reason in solving problems, directing conduct, etc., effectively."

3. "In psychology, measured success in using these abilities to perform certain tasks."

The cat meets every one of these criteria superbly.

Of course, no one who has ever played a teasing game with a cat, watched a cat figuring out how to open a cupboard, or had a cat patiently make clear that its litter box needed changing could ever doubt how powerful is its reasoning power.

The question of whether cats are more intelligent than dogs has often led to hot disputes between dog and cat fanciers. Cat lovers, as one might expect, insist that their pets are smarter (and more affectionate, in their own way) than dogs, and they have a supporter in Dr. James B. Allison, who has dealt with cats for years as director of the Bureau of Biological Research at Rutgers University. He points, for example, to the cats' cleverness in discovering how to open cages closed with a hasp and bolt. By lifting the bolt on its chain out of the hasp, the cats could open the door of their cages and escape. This clearly took a high degree of reasoning.

Some people judge animals on the basis of their ability to learn tricks. Cats can learn tricks, but it is much more difficult to teach a cat to do tricks than to train a dog. Does this indicate less intelligence? I don't think so. A cat is quick to learn anything that concerns its own welfare. It doesn't learn tricks as easily as a dog simply because it is not as docile or as eager to please. It is too independent and self-reliant for that.

But cats do learn what interests them. In Long Beach, California, there is a firehouse cat that's the first one to slide down the pole when the bells begin to clang. Other cats have learned—without being taught—how to ring doorbells to gain admittance, or to bang knockers. Most cat owners have seen their own pets trying to open a door by grabbing the doorknob, which surely shows that the cat has reasoned out the connection between the doorknob and the opening and closing of the door. Ida Mellen has written of a cat in a family with one blind member. If the cat wanted to go into the house while any other member of the family was on the porch, it simply went to the door and waited. But if only the blind person was on the porch, the cat would jump on him to let him know what it wanted.

LONGEVITY

Cats live longer, on the average, then dogs. The average lifespan of the cat used to be about twelve to fourteen years. But the advances in veterinary medicine have had the same effect on the life expectancy of the cat that human medical progress has had on man. Today the average cat, properly cared for, probably has a life expectancy of about seventeen years or more.

This life expectancy, of course, is affected by many factors. Diet is important. So is health care: trips to the veterinarian whenever any serious illness appears.

The most important question of all in determining how long a cat will live is whether it is permitted to roam freely or is confined to the house. A cat that roams at will usually has a much shorter life than its indoor friends. Sooner or later the law of averages in this automobile age catches up with it. That is the reason so many people today train their cats to use a litter box rather than go out to relieve themselves. Today, one rarely hears about putting the cat out at night.

Some amazing records for longevity have been established by well-cared-for cats. A Los Angeles cat was well into its thirty-fourth year when it died. A South African cat lived to the age of thirty-one, and so did at least one other California cat and one in Canada. A Connecticut cat lived to be twenty-eight. There have been a goodly number of cats who have lived within a year or two of that mark. And these are only the authenticated, recorded cases.

It is impossible to compare the cat's lifespan with man's. One proposed comparison held that a cat of one year was the equivalent of a child of three years and four months. But a year-old cat is an adult animal; it has probably already reproduced, if it is a stray, and it is certainly able to take care of itself. A three-year-old child, on the other hand, is still a helpless infant.

5. NUTRITION AND FEEDING

I never shall forget the indulgence with which he [Dr. Samuel Johnson] treated Hodge, his cat; for whom he himself used to go out and buy oysters, lest the servants having that trouble should take a dislike to the poor creature.

—JAMES BOSWELL (1740-1795)

A GREAT deal of nonsense is spoken and written about cats, and this is true above all in the area of nutrition and feeding. We are told that all cats love milk; that they should never be fed starch or vegetables; that fat is bad for them; that bones do them no harm.

Perhaps the silliest thing that is said about the cat is that it will, given the opportunity, instinctively choose a balanced and sensible diet.

It won't.

Most cats will choose sugar, white bread, spaghetti sauce, or some other unlikely treat, often preferring such delicacies to fresh red meat.

And yet meat is the basic food of the cat, which is a carnivore. Its natural prey includes many small animals, such as the rabbit, which are herbivorous. In eating these animals, the cat consumes everything: muscle meat, internal organs, the half-digested vegetable contents of the digestive system. In this way the cat's overall nutritional requirements are met.

But the cat that is not feral develops tastes for foods unavailable to

89

cats that have to kill their own game. It is the responsibility of the owner to see to it that the cat gets the proper kind of diet, a balanced diet that will meet all of its needs.

Until recently, that was a difficult task, for comparatively little research had been carried out on the nutritional requirements of the cat, compared with the enormous amount of information available on the dog. In recent years, however, an increasing number of scientists have begun to take an interest in this area of research. The Committee on Animal Nutrition, National Academy of Sciences-National Research Council, has finally brought together the existing knowledge on cat nutrition. This chapter is based largely on that study, prepared by Dr. S. N. Gershoff of the Department of Nutrition, Harvard School of Public Health. This is the first time that this material has been available to the cat owner.*

PROTEINS, FATS, CARBOHYDRATES

Man requires five major elements in his food: proteins, fats, carbohydrates, minerals, and vitamins. The cat needs all of these with the possible exception of carbohydrates. The need for carbohydrates has not been demonstrated, which does not mean that the need doesn't exist; it just means that we don't know. In case such a need does exist, it may be just as well to provide some in its diet, if the diet is adequate in proteins and fats.

Proteins exist in a number of forms. Each kind of protein is a combination of several of the twenty amino acids. When proteins are taken in through the digestive system, they are broken down again into their constituent amino acids, which are then reassembled in the form of new protein. Surplus amino acids are burned as energy.

Fats are broken down in the body into fatty acids and glycogen. The body then transforms glycogen into glucose, a body fuel. The

---

* I have also made substantial use of the material on the cat by Drs. Patricia P. Scott, A. Carvalho da Silva, and Marny A. Lloyd-Jacob in *The UFAW Handbook on the Care and Management of Laboratory Animals,* published by the Universities Federation for Animal Welfare of Great Britain, and of research reports appearing in American veterinary journals.

fatty acids are changed into body fats. (Generally the same course is taken by carbohydrates in man, but in a more roundabout way.)

"Most cat nutritionists favor high-fat, high-protein diets for cats," Dr. Gershoff found. "Purified diets containing twenty-five to thirty per cent fat and thirty to forty per cent protein were commonly used. These high-fat rations appear to be more palatable than low-fat diets."

The cat's requirements of proteins and fats are much higher than those of the dog. Over thirty per cent of the diet must be protein, for example, if a kitten is to grow properly; the best results are obtained when the protein content reaches forty per cent.

Cat show exhibitors should be especially interested in one finding reported in England: cats which were "maintained for three months exclusively on lean beef muscle had an extremely good appearance and especially soft fur."

On the other hand, a high-fat diet apparently enables the cat to absorb vitamin A more efficiently than it can with a low-fat intake. "This suggests that many low-fat commercial cat foods may supply inadequate vitamin A," Dr. Gershoff told a conference of veterinarians.

Cats maintained on the high-fat diet were found to accumulate a small amount of fat around the liver, unlike cats fed low-fat diets. Whether the liver fat is harmful has not been determined.

MINERALS

All animals need minerals—calcium and phosphorus to build teeth and bones; iron, copper, and cobalt to produce healthy blood; other elements for the development and maintenance of all the nerves, muscles, and organs of the body.

The exact amounts of these minerals needed by the cat have not been determined. Until we know otherwise, it must be assumed that the cat needs reasonable quantities of the minerals, in roughly the same proportion, say, as man and the dog.

The effect of mineral deficiencies has been studied. It was found that kittens fed only raw or cocked heart—a diet particularly deficient in calcium and iodine—showed undesirable effects after seven weeks.

These effects included nervousness, inability to coordinate, and finally paralysis of the hind legs. The bones softened and then collapsed, causing the paralysis. The thyroid was affected and so were the kidneys.

When calcium was added to heart in the diet of kittens, the bones did not soften and the thyroid was not affected as it had been. Adding iodine strengthened the thyroid and delayed the weakening of the bones.

A unique problem in considering the cat's mineral needs is the unusual susceptibility of the cat to kidney and bladder stones. There has often been speculation that high-mineral diets might be a factor in this. But several nutritionists were unable to cause urinary stones in kittens even with diets containing as much as thirty per cent minerals.

VITAMINS

These accessory organic substances are needed for metabolism. They are essential to life and growth. The cat's needs for these vitamins are not necessarily the same as man's.

VITAMIN A: The human body manufactures this vitamin mostly from carotene, but the cat does not, at least not in important quantities. Cats whose diet is deficient in vitamin A lose their appetites and become emaciated. Some show weakness of the hind leg with some signs of stiffness. There are scaly changes in the tissues of several of the organs. The lungs often become inflamed. So do the eyes. The teeth are affected adversely. The hearing and the nervous system are impaired.

Acute deficiencies of vitamin A usually result in death.

Fat in the diet helps the cat to utilize fat-soluble vitamin A, so it is important that there be enough fat in the cat's food.

NIACIN: This is the antipellagra factor in the vitamin B complex. A lack of it in cats results in a feline disease resembling pellagra. The cat suffers diarrhea, emaciation, and death. Often a respiratory disease precedes death. Of forty-five cats used in one experiment, not one lived more than twenty days on a diet without niacin.

FOLIC ACID: Another B complex factor, this vitamin causes

anemia and a sharp drop in white corpuscles when it is absent from the cat's body.

CHOLINE: Also lumped in the B complex, the lack of this vitamin in cats causes weight loss and fatty livers.

THIAMINE (B_1): A cat whose diet provides an insufficient amount of thiamine may suffer from loss of appetite, vomiting, inability to coordinate, abnormal reflexes, convulsions, and heart disorders. One team of researchers found that cats fed raw carp or herring ultimately displayed a thiamine deficiency, but cats fed raw perch, catfish, butterfish, did not.

RIBOFLAVIN (B_2): Cats suffering from the lack of this vitamin lose their appetites, fade away to skin and bones, and finally die. The hair, particularly around the head, sometimes falls out. Cataracts have been observed in chronically deficient cats. Impaired nerve function, digestive disturbance, anemia, sore mouth, poor litters, and poor nursing of kittens have also been reported as results of riboflavin deficiencies.

If the cat's diet is high in carbohydrates, its need for riboflavin is slightly lessened. The reason for this, it appears, is that more riboflavin is manufactured in the cat's intestines when the intake of carbohydrates is high.

PYRIDOXINE (B_6): The deficiency of this vitamin in cats is characterized by stunted growth, emaciation, convulsions (the nervous system is affected), anemia, kidney disease, and deposits of iron in the liver.

ASCORBIC ACID (C): Apparently vitamin C is not required by cats.

VITAMIN D: Rickets, as one might suppose, is the result of a lack of vitamin D in cats, just as in man. For that reason this vitamin, which is essential to the utilization of calcium and phosphorus in forming teeth and bones, is especially needed by the pregnant queen and the growing kitten. The requirement of vitamin D for cats over a year and a half old is believed to be quite low.

VITAMIN E: One effect of an insufficient supply of vitamin E may be steatitis, an extremely painful disease in cats; it can be fatal. (See a discussion of this in the section on commercial cat foods below.)

Vitamin E deficiency also can cause lost litters, sickly kittens, and a drop in the red blood cells.

VITAMIN K: The need of the cat for this vitamin has not been established.

PANTOTHENIC ACID: Loss of weight and fatty livers are among the ill effects that follow upon an inadequate supply of this vitamin.

CALORIES AND ENERGY

A kitten's caloric requirements are, proportionately, a great deal higher than an adult cat's. The kitten must burn up enormous amounts of energy just producing all the cells that enable it to grow. On top of that, kittens usually play harder than grown-up, sensible cats. It has been noted that a growing cat consumes about eighty calories per pound of body weight every day.

Around the time that kittens are weaned, they need about 125 calories a day per pound of body weight. This drops off as the kitten grows. By the time it is thirty weeks old—about seven or eight months —the kitten needs only about 65 calories per pound of body weight per day.

The adult cat's caloric requirements depend on the kind of life it leads, just as with humans. They also depend on the weather, to some extent, particularly with cats that are permitted out of the house to roam. From the time it is a year old, the cat that goes out for its exercise, chases rabbits, is chased by dogs, and climbs into trees (for firemen to rescue) needs 40 to 45 calories per pound of body weight every day.

Dr. Mark L. Morris, a well-known specialist in animal nutrition, has found that temperature changes have an average effect of about 46 per cent on food consumption. Outdoor cats tend to eat a good deal more heavily at the onset of cold weather in the fall and gain extra weight. However, the food consumption tapers off even though the weather remains cold. The reverse of this process takes place in the spring.

The sedentary cat—and that includes most pet cats, living wholly in apartments or houses, sleeping a considerable portion of the day, playing only briefly, exercising hardly at all—needs substantially fewer calories, in the neighborhood of 30 calories a day per pound of body weight.

A word may be appropriate here regarding obesity. Overweight is less common a problem in cats than in dogs—and far less than in man. The average female cat's weight is between six and ten pounds; the average male's, eight to fifteen. (There are authentic records of cats that have weighed as much as thirty-five pounds!)

Obviously the simplest way to bring down a cat's weight is to cut down its food supply. Unlike its master or mistress, the cat can't sneak fattening treats that aren't on its diet, so a weight-reducing diet almost always is effective. If your cat is sedentary and weighs fifteen pounds, and you want to get its weight down to about ten pounds, figure the number of calories it would require to sustain itself at the ten-pound level, and make that the daily ration. It may also be helpful to add vitamin B complex as a supplement to the diet.

COOKED OR UNCOOKED?

There are few arguments concerning cat care that can arouse greater passions on the part of some fanciers than the question of whether the cat's food should be cooked or uncooked.

There are some foods, of course, that everyone agrees must be cooked—pork, for one, because the muscle worms that cause trichinosis in man can also kill the cat. And it's generally agreed that fish should be cooked, too. But after that, the arguments begin.

The National Research Council's survey of technical knowledge about cat nutrition examined two studies of the comparative values of cooked and uncooked foods for cats. The survey summarized the reports of these experiments: "Consistently better growth, development, reproduction, and lactation were obtained when raw meat and milk were fed to cats than when they received cooked meat and milk."

Moreover, once the "deficiency state" resulting from the cooked diet "was produced in kittens, it could not be reversed. When deficient adult cats were returned to a raw diet, normal animals were not produced for several generations."

Now, these results must be viewed with a great deal of caution. The diet itself—meat and milk—was something less than ideal. How would those cats have managed on a good canned cat food or dog food? Would vitamin-mineral supplements have had any material effect on the results? Until those questions are answered, it is best to consider this whole matter of cooking like this:

If you are feeding your cat fresh meat, let it be raw. If you are feeding the cat a canned (which means cooked) food or some other precooked food, make sure it meets all the nutritional requirements listed above.

MEAT

BEEF: Excellent. The best for the cat is muscle meat. Feed it in small chunks or ground. Once a week the muscle meat might be varied with organ meats: "lights" (lungs), heart, tripe, kidneys, or liver. Some veterinarians insist the liver should be cooked.

HORSEMEAT: Good, but fat must be added.

VEAL: Many cats prefer this to beef. Either the muscle meat or the organs will do nicely.

LAMB: It's too expensive to serve your cat the chops, unless you're an unusually generous master, but the kidneys are very good and they are a convenient size for purchasing. Cut up in one-inch cubes, lamb kidney is almost a sure-fire cure of a jaded feline appetite.

PORK: Trimmed of fat, ground, and cooked, pork may make a pleasant change of diet for the cat.

FISH AND CHICKEN

Fish once a week is a treat and it's good for the cat. It must be cooked, preferably steamed to retain as many of the nutrients as possible. And it must be carefully boned. Even canned fish that's labeled "boneless" sometimes has wicked little spears in it, so be careful.

Shellfish are perfectly acceptable, too, but it's a waste of money—the cat will appreciate mackerel just as much.

Chicken is good for the cat, and most cats love it. (Turkey, too.) Be sure it's cooked, however, and that there are no bones to catch in the cat's throat. One more caution: do *not* let the cat have the skin of the chicken or the turkey. The cat can't digest the skin easily, and it can irritate its digestive system by trying.

OTHER FOODS

MILK: A great many cats cannot tolerate milk and some of those who can keep it down can't stand the sight of the stuff. One effect that milk has on many cats is cathartic. When milk is given to a cat, it should always be lukewarm.

CHEESE: Occasional servings of cream cheese and cottage cheese are approved by many veterinarians. My own cats love all kinds of cheese, but they don't get them for dinner.

EGGS: Ideally, the cat should get the yolk of a one-minute boiled egg twice a week or more often. It can be mixed with milk or with the cat's other food.

VEGETABLES: Green vegetables, in small quantities, are good for the cat. They can be cooked or raw. If you want to give the cat a treat, get some oat seeds and plant them in a flower box in a sunny corner of the kitchen. The cat will be delighted at the opportunity to eat the green, growing grass. But it won't keep the cat away from your philodendrons, unfortunately.

POTATOES: It has long been an article of faith with many cat lovers that no cat should ever be fed any starch, and particularly potatoes. The theory was that the cat couldn't digest starch. But it can be digested by the cat, provided it is broken in texture before it is ingested. This means the potatoes should be cooked and mashed. Cooked, mashed potatoes were an important part of one of the experimental diets cited by the National Research Council.

WATER: The cat needs water to drink. Some owners who give their cats milk think water is unnecessary. They're wrong—milk is a food, and it's not to be used as a substitute for water. A dish of clean, fresh water should be on the floor, available to the cat, at all times.

COMMERCIAL CAT FOODS

There is a variety of cat food available in pet shops and super-markets. Today pet foods outsell baby foods in grocery stores throughout the country. Most of this merchandise is of excellent quality—which doesn't necessarily mean it's the best thing for your cat—and is carefully prepared in order to give your cat most of the substances it needs in its diet.

Can you simply open a can of cat food and give it to your pet—and know that it is getting the nutrients it needs? The National Research Council survey answered that question with these words: "Much of the commercial cat food is nutritionally inadequate and must be supplemented with other foods."

It will be noted that *all* commercial cat foods are not lumped in the "inadequate" category, from which fact it can be assumed that some prepared foods are properly nutritious.

This puts the burden on the cat owner to study carefully the labels on available foods. Every label must list ingredients and an analysis of the contents. The ingredients and the analysis should be compared with the requirements listed below.

In general, the cat owner is well advised to alternate a carefully chosen canned food—and don't overlook the dog foods when you're selecting it—with fresh meat.

THE CANNED FISH PROBLEM: An unresolved conflict exists among scientists regarding the dangers of canned fish as the exclusive element in a cat's diet. Until this matter is resolved to everyone's satisfaction, cat owners ought to exercise extreme caution in feeding canned fish to their pets. This is particularly important because several cat foods make a point of advertising that they are all fish.

There have been six reports from research teams that cats fed exclusively or almost exclusively on canned cat food consisting entirely of fish contracted a disease called *steatitis*. In most—but not all—of these cases the fish was red meat tuna. (Because other fish packs were involved, however, the findings ought to be applied to any all-fish cat foods.)

Steatitis is an agonizingly painful disease. The fatty layer just under

NUTRITION AND FEEDING

SATISFACTORY LEVELS OF NUTRIENTS
TO MEET THE NUTRITIONAL REQUIREMENTS
OF THE GROWING CAT

NUTRIENT	PER POUND OF DIET[1]
Total proteins	4.6 ounces
Minerals	Required
Vitamins	
Vitamin A	Required
Vitamin D	Required
Vitamin E (international units)	(34)[2]
Vitamin K	—[3]
Thiamine	4 milligrams
Riboflavin	(4)
Vitamin B₆	4 milligrams
Niacin	40 milligrams
Pantothenic Acid	(5)
Biotin	—
Folic Acid	Not required
Choline	—
Vitamin B₁₂	—
Inositol	—

[1] The values that are not in parentheses are estimated from various adequate rations, hence are probably in excess of the actual requirement.
The values in parentheses are tentative estimates of the minimal requirement and contain no margins of safety.
[2] Not satisfactory if excessive dietary source of polyunsaturated fatty acids is fed.
[3] Signifies no information is available on a qualitative requirement.

the skin becomes inflamed; the cat displays "exquisite tenderness," as *The Merck Veterinary Manual* puts it, "manifest by resentment" when it is touched on the back or the abdomen. The animal loses its agility; it is reluctant to move at all. The cat becomes feverish and loses its appetite. As the disease progresses, the lightest touch is enough to make the cat cry out with pain. The disease often ends in death.

Why canned all-fish cat food causes steatitis is still not definitely known. When the association of the food with the disease was first observed, it was believed that absence of vitamin E from the diet was

99

responsible. Almost all of the companies packing all-fish cat foods quickly enriched the food with alphatocopherol, one of four forms of vitamin E, and slapped "added vitamin E" labels on the cans.

But a team of researchers at Angell Memorial Animal Hospital at Boston then reported on eight more cases of steatitis traceable to canned all-fish cat food—and four of these had been fed from cans labeled "added vitamin E."

It seemed that the addition of vitamin E was not the answer—at least, not the entire answer—to the problem. Then Danish scientists, studying the same disease in minks, came to the conclusion that "yellow fat," as steatitis is sometimes called, "is primarily due to the contents of marine fat in the feed." They decided that "the most satisfactory method of preventing 'yellow fat' . . . is control of the fat composition in feeds, so that the content of marine fat does not exceed three to four per cent."

The picture is still unclear, for a new report from an American source says that cats in *its* experiments were completely protected against steatitis by the addition of vitamin E to a fish diet.

As an additional complication, Dr. Morris, in his manual on *Nutrition and Diet in Small Animal Medicine,* warns: "The possibility of alphatocopherol containing a toxic factor for cats should be considered. In the preparation of experimental rations for cats, we added excessive amounts of alphatocopherol to the diet. This substance was very unpalatable to cats and the animals would actually starve unless alphatocopherol was removed or added at a much reduced level."

This raises some question as to whether *enough* vitamin E can be added to canned fish to protect the cat consumer.

The only conclusion that can be stated at this time is this: If your cat likes canned all-fish cat food, feed it only such food if it is labeled "added vitamin E." But give the cat this food only once a week. The rest of the time feed it foods that do not include fish.

SUPPLEMENTS

Everything that has been said in this chapter up to this point should make clear that it is not as simple as it might at first appear to ensure your cat a balanced diet with the proper intake of vitamins and minerals.

This problem becomes more acute when the cat is sick, pregnant, lactating, or growing.

Nevertheless, some authorities believe it is unnecessary to add extra vitamins or minerals to the diet. They meet disagreement from other experts who think vitamin-mineral supplements make good sense.

I'm inclined to agree with the latter group. There is a very slight danger of overdosing the cat, but this is so remote as to be unimportant in our considerations. On the other hand, a vitamin-mineral supplement is a kind of insurance that your cat is getting the proper amount of these two essential kinds of nutrient.

However, it is necessary to be cautious about the vitamin-mineral supplement that is used. One of the supplements most popular with pet owners, for example, provides a seriously inadequate supply of pantothenic acid. The formulas should be compared with the table of nutrients on page 99.

Vitamin-mineral supplements for cats come in many forms: drops, capsules, pills, powders, and small pellets designed to be highly palatable to animals. Supplements intended for use by humans can be used, if you prefer.

KITTEN FEEDING

The feeding of kittens under the age of five weeks will be discussed in Chapter 9. Here the subject under consideration will be the kitten from weaning to adulthood.

About the time the kitten is five or six weeks old, it can begin to get its first food as a supplement to the milk it obtains nursing. This early food can be a prepared cereal for human babies or a preparation devised especially for kittens. The latter is preferable; it is much higher in protein than pablum for babies (thirty per cent as against fifteen per cent). This is an important point, for kittens grow at a much faster rate than human babies, and so they need a bigger proportion of tissue-building protein. Whichever kind of cereal is used, it should be moistened with warmed milk or with evaporated milk diluted with water.

If the kitten has difficulty taking this food from a spoon at first, stick your finger in the cereal and then let the kitten suck it off your finger as though it were a nipple.

Feed this to the kitten three or four times a day, and let it continue to nurse in between.

After a week or two, it's time for the next step in weaning. Now strained meats of the kind prepared for human babies should be added to the diet. The strained meats should be warmed, of course—everything fed to the kitten should be warmed.

Scraped meats are added to the diet next, then twice-ground lean meat, finally boneless canned fish, finely broken up. The meals can then look something like this:

> MORNING: Warmed milk with a barely cooked egg and baby cereal mixed into it. Vitamin-mineral drops.
> FORENOON: Strained baby meats mixed with baby cereal.
> NOON: Scraped or doubly chopped raw lean meat.
> AFTERNOON: Warmed milk and egg again.
> EVENING: Baby strained meats or doubly chopped raw lean meat.
> NIGHT: Baby strained meats or doubly chopped raw lean meat.

The meals should be cut down to four a day as soon as the kitten begins to show a diminished interest in the frequent feedings. As the baby teeth appear, more solid food can be added: meat softened and cut into tiny cubes, fish carefully boned and mashed, and so on.

In the fourth month, the meals can be reduced to three. After that, two meals a day should be sufficient.

The average kitten weighs slightly more than three ounces at birth. It can be expected to gain about an ounce every three days until it is seven weeks old; it then weighs about twenty ounces. In the next month it will probably gain another ten ounces. The weight will gradually increase month by month—by ten ounces, then by eleven ounces, by twelve ounces, and so on. The top of the growth curve is reached in the ninth month. Then the monthly gain in weight begins to fall off very gradually for the next five months.

NUTRITION AND FEEDING

ADULT FEEDING

Many cat owners feed their full-grown pets twice a day. There is nothing wrong in this, but it is unnecessary. Barring unusual conditions, one meal a day is sufficient for almost all cats.

About four to seven ounces of food a day will sustain the average cat very well. In the adult cat the stomach will hold four and a half ounces of food or more. At one feeding the cat can take in quite enough food to keep it comfortably occupied for the next twenty-four hours.

It is well to serve the food in a bowl on the floor—with a generous supply of paper under the dish, for cats love to drag morsels of food out of their dish onto the floor, for no reason that I've ever been able to determine.

The food should be put down for the cat at about the same time every day, for cats are creatures of habit, and essentially conservative. If the cat hasn't eaten its food within a reasonable time—say, half an hour—and shows no interest in it, take it up. *Never leave food down for the cat!* When food is left out for the cat, it attracts insects, dries out so that it is completely unappetizing to the cat, and simply bores the poor cat, who gets sick of the sight of it.

Whether the cat really needs variety in its food is something that nobody really knows. On general principles, it seems no harm to give the cat a change of dish for a day or two now and then.

Sometimes a cat is a fussy eater. Usually this is because it has not been fed in the proper manner in the past—most often because its food has been left down for it all day.

Feeding the cat by hand for a day or two, or petting it while it eats, may induce it to eat properly, especially if its food is set out for it only for a short time each day.

If that doesn't start the cat eating, a meal of diced lamb kidneys will usually stimulate the most listless appetite.

If the cat absolutely refuses to eat anything but food which is not good for it, its food—its proper diet—should be set out for it every day nevertheless. When the cat refuses to eat, the food should be taken up. This should be done until the cat eats. This can be quite a strain on the owner's nerves, for the cat may very well starve itself for a week before surrendering, but surrender it will, in time.

In persistent or recurring cases of inappetence, it is wise to consult your veterinarian. Judicious prescription of vitamins sometimes can help with such problems.

One last word about the feeding of the adult cat: there are several companies which manufacture special formulas of canned cat foods for the feeding of cats with special dietary problems. These foods are available only on prescription from a veterinarian. If he recommends such a food, his advice should be followed carefully.

SNACKS AND TIDBITS

If a cat has been eating its meals properly, there is no reason why it should be denied snacks from time to time—but only if its appetite for regular meals is good. Little treats, especially prepared to be palatable to cats, are available in pet shops and supermarkets. They are the best tidbits your pet can eat.

Other snacks do no harm. My cats all love cheese, for example, and they're all hearty eaters. So, when I have cheese, they have cheese— tiny little pieces, of course. They also like a little cake, cookies, bread, meat, chili (terrible thing to give a cat!), curried rice (ditto), and so on.

THE LAST WORD

Remember, above all, that your cat is not the best judge of what he should eat. The National Research Council survey summed it up this way: "Some foods of high acceptability were found to be nutritionally inadequate when used over extended periods."

DAILY FEEDING SCHEDULE

AGE	FROM 5 TO 9 WEEKS	FROM 9 WEEKS TO 4 MONTHS	FROM 4 MONTHS TO 1 YEAR	OVER 1 YEAR
Number of feedings	4	3	2	1 or 2

6. THE KITTEN

The playful kitten, with its pretty little tigerish gambols, is infinitely more amusing than half the people one is obliged to live with in the world.

—LADY SYDNEY MORGAN (1783-1859)

EVEN cat haters often like kittens. It would be a cold heart indeed that could resist one of these fluffy, playful, pretty, coy, silly, and utterly charming little creatures.

Sometimes kittens are too attractive for their own good. A person who doesn't like cats will be so taken by a kitten occasionally that he'll take the kitten into his home—only to abandon it when it grows into a cat.

Presumably, a person capable of this kind of callousness would not be reading this book, however, so it can be taken for granted that your kitten will grow into a cat. How healthy, happy, and congenial a cat, may depend to a considerable extent on the care you give it as a kitten.

Regardless of its age, the kitten's first and most urgent need is for love. It's a baby. It's just left its warm mother and its brothers and sisters. It has probably been enclosed in a box or a carrying case for the first, frightening time in its young life. Chances are that it's had its first automobile ride. It is suddenly in the midst of strange, new surroundings.

You can't set the kitten down and then walk off and leave it to its own devices. What the kitten needs at this stage is a warm lap, caressing hands, and soft, reassuring voices. Then, as it begins to show

105

an interest in its surroundings, it can be introduced to all the humans in the house. It can be permitted to explore its new home.

If the kitten's had a long, as well as an exciting, day, it may prefer, as most babies would, to go to sleep instead. It may be so worn out that it will sleep for the better part of a day or two. There's nothing to worry if it does sleep that long, unless the kitten shows signs of illness.

A REMINDER

In Chapter 3, many of the initial problems that a cat presents to its new owners were discussed, including introductions to babies and to dogs, equipment, examination by a veterinarian, and sleeping accommodations. If you've forgotten what was said there, it might be a good idea to glance over that chapter again and refresh your memory.

CHOOSING A VETERINARIAN

Even before you acquire your kitten—if that's possible—it's well to decide on the veterinarian to whom you're going to take the cat.

If you haven't had a pet before, you may be in for a surprise. The old-time "horse doctor" is a thing of the past. Today's veterinarian is a professionally educated physician, surgeon, dentist, psychiatrist, gynecologist, obstetrician, allergist, orthopedist, ophthalmologist, endocrinologist, neurologist, and pathologist, all in one. No general practitioner in human medicine must be skilled in so many areas and specialties of medical science. To prepare for this mission, the veterinarian must pass through training that closely resembles that of the doctor of medicine.

Nevertheless, in veterinary as in human medicine, there are doctors and there are doctors. Not all men will be equally talented, equally intelligent, equally devoted to their responsibilities. The average veterinarian will be a man to whom you can gratefully and confidently entrust the care of your pet. But if you want to find a superior veterinarian—or if you want to avoid one of the few inferior vets—then you'll have to give some thought to the matter.

One good way to find out about vets is to talk to some of the people who are their clients—dog owners, cat owners, dog breeders, cat breeders. The last two groups are likely to be better informed than the usual pet owner. However, you're almost bound to get contradictory opinions and will have to exercise your own judgment on what you hear.

On your first visit to the vet's office, you'll be able to form your own opinion of him. Don't pay too much attention to his manner of dealing with you—at the vet's office it's the cat who's the patient, not you. If he is somewhat curt and disinclined to listen to your stories about the cute things that kitten does, remember that he's a busy man with other patients waiting. If he's brusque, it's probably because a lifetime of watching people neglect their animals by failing to follow veterinary advice has left him somewhat disillusioned about man.

Watch closely how he handles the animal patients. The good vet may sometimes appear very firm with animals, but he never *needlessly* inflicts pain. His confidence in himself and his knowledge are apparent. He should be relaxed in his examination of the animal. Personally, I have never trusted a vet who shows any fear of a dog or a cat.

The vet's examining room, operating room, and equipment are also good clues to his ability and his attitude toward his profession. Obviously, a vet with a practice in a low-income neighborhood is likely to have a less impressive office than a Park Avenue vet. But both should have examining rooms that are clean, neat, and professional in appearance.

While you are giving the vet a looking-over, remember that he's undoubtedly sizing up you, too. And vets tend to put pet owners into two groups: those who take care of their animals by following instructions, no matter how much inconvenience or effort may be involved, and those who expect the vet to perform miracles—who neglect the pet until its problems are advanced and complicated, but won't do as the vet suggests because it's too much trouble.

You have the right to expect the vet to explain your pet's problems fully in language you can understand. He has the right to expect your cooperation.

On your visit to the vet, you must tell him that you've just acquired the kitten and you want it thoroughly examined. He'll check its eyes, its hearing, its teeth, its bone structure, its general health and development. And he'll be able to give you sound advice on the care of the cat.

FORMULA FOR THE NURSING KITTEN

It's best to get a kitten that's at least eight weeks old and already weaned, or ready to be weaned. But if, by some unfortunate circumstance, you find yourself suddenly saddled with all the responsibilities that a mother cat normally has, you'd better be prepared for your maternal role.

If you're lucky—and you probably won't be—you may be able to find a mother cat in the neighborhood who's still nursing her young. It's far more likely that you'll have to prepare the milk yourself.

The problem will be to approximate cat's milk for the nursing kitten. This may require more thought than you might suppose. For the nutritional needs of the cat, as we have seen, are quite different from those of other animals and of humans.

Let's take a look at the composition of various milks:

	CAT	DOG	COW	HUMAN	GOAT	SHEEP
WATER	82.0	75.1	87.0	87.4	86.8	84.0
PROTEIN	7.0	8.4	3.4	1.3	3.7	5.0
SUGAR	5.0	3.2	4.9	7.0	4.6	4.0
FAT	5.0	9.8	3.8	3.5	4.0	4.0
ASH	0.6	0.7	0.7	0.2	0.8	0.9

A study of these percentages indicates some lines of thought. Obviously, cow's milk will not be an adequate substitute for cat's milk; the protein content is far too low. For the same reason, a formula that might be used in preparing a human baby's bottle won't give a kitten the nutrient values it needs.

The only other milk that is close to cat's milk is that of the dog, which is higher in protein, fat, and ash, although it is lower in water (which need not trouble us unduly) and in sugar.

This is one formula for foster feeding of *puppies:*

1 cup of whole homogenized vitamin D milk

1 egg yolk

1 teaspoon lime water

1 teaspoon of dextrose

Adapting this for *kittens,* we might increase the dextrose to two teaspoons. Otherwise, it should be perfectly suitable for the orphaned kitten.

There are also commercial preparations for bitch's milk that are acceptable and convenient, but a trifle expensive.

The formula should be fed to the kitten at body temperature. In the cat, this means 101.5 degrees Fahrenheit, give or take a degree. Testing it on the wrist, as parents do with a baby's bottle, is an easy way to check the temperature.

The bottle and nipples should be sterilized, of course, for kittens are as susceptible to germs as babies are. The nipples may give some slight difficulty in the first week. The nipples for human babies may be too big. In that case, a doll's bottle and nipples, which are smaller, may prove helpful. As a last resort, try an old, clean handkerchief, twisted to a point, dipped in milk and then inserted in the kitten's mouth. This never fails.

A kitten can take about seven c.c.s (cubic centimeters) of formula —or a little more—five times a day. A teaspoon, for comparative purposes, is about four c.c.s. One sign that the kitten has had enough milk at a feeding is the bubbles of milk that appear at its mouth. If it stops sucking, it might be full, lazy, or forgetful—you'll have to decide which.

When the kitten is through feeding, jiggle it gently and pat it on the back to burp it. Then take a soft synthetic sponge, moistened with lukewarm water, and rub its abdomen and the area around its anus. Rub the abdomen gently but repeatedly, and always toward the hindquarters. This is what the mother cat does with her tongue after the kittens have nursed. They are unable to urinate and defecate by themselves; she must help them, and in her absence this task is yours.

It is well to do this away from the kitten's bed, to avoid soiling it. After the massaging, when the kitten has eliminated its wastes, it is necessary to clean away carefully all urine and feces from its body. After a week or two this sort of thing will no longer be necessary. It will be apparent when the kitten is able to carry out these functions on its own.

The entire procedure—warming formula, feeding kitten, burping, massaging, and cleaning—should be performed approximately every two hours during the kitten's first week. If the prescribed method is followed, and the kitten is basically healthy, it should survive, although you may not.

At the beginning of the second week, you can begin giving the kitten a little more at each feeding, and the feedings can then be three hours apart. You'll really enjoy that extra hour.

EYES AND TEETH

At first the kitten won't be able to see. Between the eighth and the twelfth day its eyes will open. But it will be another day or two until they can coordinate their muscles and nerves and optic mechanisms in such a way as actually to see. And until they are nearly a month old they should not be exposed to strong, direct sunlight or to an unshaded electric light bulb.

Often the eyelids will begin to stick together a day or two after the eyes have opened. This is caused simply by the normal secretion from the eyes. Moisten a piece of cotton with warm water and rub it gently along the eye from the nose outward. As the crystallized secretion begins to soften, the cotton can be moved up and down across the eyelids until they are ready to separate. Then the eyes should be dried with sterile cotton. Your veterinarian can recommend an ophthalmic solution that should clear up the condition quickly.

The teeth, too, do not become operative at once. They are in the kitten's jaw, but buried under the gums. The kitten begins to cut its deciduous ("baby") teeth at about eleven days. By the fourth or fifth week all twenty-six of these are in place. As in human children, these teeth are later pushed out of the gum to make way for the adult teeth. This process can begin as early as the fourth month or as late as the seventh; the usual time is about the sixth month.

The teething process, as all parents know, can be a trying period. The kitten often works up a mild fever at this time. It may appear to have some difficulty in eating.

Occasionally the milk teeth show some stubbornness about dropping out, and the adult teeth may begin to grow in beside them. For this reason, it's well for the owner to examine the kitten's mouth every few days while it's teething. At the first sign of trouble, the kitten should be taken to the veterinarian, who can remove the obstinate baby teeth, thus permitting the adult teeth to move into their proper places.

If the kitten undergoes a painful teething, its appetite may drop off. Your vet can suggest a nontoxic local anesthetic that can be applied to the gums to ease the pain and thus make eating more inviting. At this crucial stage in the kitten's development, you cannot permit its intake of food to fall off, for now, of all times, it needs vitamins, tissue-building protein, and bone-building minerals if it is to have sound teeth and bones.

There is one other—fortunately rare—problem that can occur in the teething kitten: fits. If this should occur, try to get the kitten into a darkened room, but don't try to control it or touch it; you'll only risk a bite, for no good reason. Instead, telephone your vet immediately. (The fit could also be caused by worms. This possibility will be discussed later in this chapter.)

BATHING

A healthy, happy kitten keeps itself clean, but it should be encouraged and assisted by regular brushing on your part. Not that the kitten will be grateful for your brushing it. On the contrary, although the kitten probably will enjoy the brushing while it is going on, it will be certain that you have dirtied its fur. As soon as you're through brushing, the kitten will begin cleaning itself.

Unless you specifically receive a recommendation to the contrary from your vet, *do not bathe your kitten!* Bathing should be a last resort, employed only in dire emergency. If the kitten falls into a filthy or foul-smelling mess, of course, a bath is unavoidable. In that event, put a drop of mineral oil in each of the kitten's eyes and put a daub of cotton in each ear, to protect those delicate organs from the soap. Your pet shop or druggist may stock shampoos especially prepared for cats. If not, use as mild a shampoo as possible, such as those sold for use on babies. Rinse and dry the kitten thoroughly and keep it out of drafts.

CLAWS

Unless the claws are clipped, they will grow too long and begin to curve into wicked little hooks. But clipping a kitten's, or cat's, nails takes a little thought and care.

It's best to approach this, if you can, as a two-man job, although one very agile person can manage it alone. Have another person hold the cat from the back, with the person's arms about the cat's midsection. While the front claws are being trimmed, the hind legs should be held, so the cat can't strike out with the hind claws. The front paws are restrained while the hind claws are being trimmed.

Have at hand a pair of fingernail clippers. Take the paw in hand and put pressure from two fingers on the top and bottom of the paw, thus forcing the claws out of their sheaths. Your light should be strong enough to shine through the claw. Look at the claw carefully. You will see a pink area in the middle of the claw. This is the quick; *you must be careful not to cut into it.* The cat's quick is as sensitive to pain as the quick under your nails. Cut the claw back close to the quick.

If you should, by some mischance, cut into the quick, you'll find that the bleeding does not stop quickly, for this is fed by a vein. The best way to stop the bleeding is by dabbing the bleeding claw with a piece of cotton dipped in Monsel's solution. Incidentally, a small bottle of Monsel's solution should be kept in the house for just such emergencies. (The man in the house will find it is better than a styptic pencil for stopping the bleeding when he's cut himself shaving.) Monsel's solution, known under its technical designation as ferric subsulphate solution, can be obtained from your pharmacist.

112

Clipping the cat's nails will prevent scratches on your hands and cut down on damage to furniture and rugs. A scratching post also will help with this problem, especially if you get the kitten early and train it to use the post. Scratching posts are made in horizontal and vertical forms; the latter are the better. The post is usually a piece of wood covered with bark or catnip-impregnated fabric. One excellent scratching post is made of cork; the cats love it.

DECLAWING

If a kitten or a cat becomes really destructive toward furniture, and a few problem cats do, there is one drastic remedy available—declawing. The entire claws are removed surgically, roots and all, so that they never grow again. The operation is performed under anesthesia.

Declawing, the technical term for which is *onychectomy*, is a controversial procedure. It is so hotly disputed that two very respected leaders in the cat fancy have offered a reward for the "arrest and conviction" of anyone who has been responsible for declawing a cat. Declawing is *not* against the law, of course. These people believe sincerely that it should be outlawed.

I disagree. One of my four cats is declawed, and it enjoys a full, happy, and secure life without its claws. Many people who love cats but fear the damage that cats can do sometimes to furniture and rugs go through life without cats for that reason. Occasionally a cat will be taken to a vet to be put to sleep because it has been guilty of so much damage with its claws. Declawing solves this problem.

Of course, declawing creates certain problems and imposes new responsibilities on the owner. A declawed cat can defend itself, but not as well as a cat with claws; it can climb trees if the customary procedure of only removing the front claws is followed, but it can't climb with the ease of an untouched cat; it can capture its prey— and sometimes just as well as the cat with claws. Because its abilities are diminished to some extent, however, the declawed cat must expect special care from its owner. I do not believe that a declawed cat should be permitted out to roam at will. There is no question that the

113

hazards to its life are greater. Otherwise, the declawed cat enjoys life every bit as much as it did before its operation.

Declawing should not be resorted to until every attempt has been made to correct the cat's objectionable habits by training. This means that the cat will usually be nearly full-grown before being declawed.

The cat displays surprisingly few signs of discomfort after the operation. For twenty-four hours, sterile dressings are maintained on the paws. But very quickly the cat is walking on its paws, despite the recent surgery, with no indication of sensitivity.

In time, the paw hardens a good deal, apparently as a result of the declawing. The cat uses it more often then as a hand. My declawed cat can make tight, formidable little fists out of her declawed paws and she slugs with those fists like a prizefighter, as the other cats have learned to their sorrow.

WINDOW SITTING

One difficulty experienced by declawed cats—and cats with claws as well—has to do with windowsills. When a cat jumps to a windowsill, it extends its claws to grab the surface better. A declawed cat has a harder time stopping its skid across the sill.

This is a real hazard to an apartment cat. Hundreds of cats are killed every year in New York City alone in falls from apartment windowsills. We always assume that the cat's judgment of distance and ability to stop is well-nigh perfect. It isn't. If the sill is smooth, and most sills are, the cat—claws or no—slides right off the sill, to plummet to the concrete below. If there is a fire escape, the cat often will try to jump to the railing of it. It will succeed, too, forty-nine out of fifty times. The fiftieth time the cat proves that it has only one life, not nine, as it misjudges the distance, goes off balance, teeters briefly, and then plunges into space.

Don't trust your cat's judgment in such matters. Keep screens on your windows and don't let the cat out on the fire escape. If the cat leans against the screen and causes it to bulge, a narrow strip of wood can be nailed across the frame.

THE KITTEN

INOCULATIONS

Two of the diseases commonly encountered in kittens—pneumonitis and feline distemper—can usually be warded off by vaccines. Both diseases will be discussed at some length in Chapter 8. Here it is enough to say that kittens are especially vulnerable to these diseases.

A serum that offers protection for about two weeks is available against feline distemper, and this may be worth considering if the kitten is about to be exposed to cats that may be carrying the disease.

There are vaccines against both feline distemper and pneumonitis. The inoculations are usually made when the kitten is about three months old. The distemper vaccine is given in two injections two weeks apart.

Many vets feel that these vaccines have not yet been developed to a sufficiently satisfactory point to warrant their use. They feel the protection is still inadequate. On the other hand, an unvaccinated kitten is exposed to disease every time you bring another cat into the house.

In this perplexing situation, the best course to follow is that prescribed by your own vet.

WORMING

Parasitism in the kitten usually concerns us most in respect to worms. Cats are involuntary hosts to several forms of worm: tapeworms, roundworms, hookworms, muscle worms, heart worms, and eye worms.

EYE WORMS: These parasites, designated *Thelazia californiensis,* are uncommon. When they are found, it is usually in the Pacific Coast states. The worms are found in the cat as well as in man, the dog, the coyote, the deer, the sheep, and the black bear. Tiny, threadlike worms of the Nematodes order, they can be seen moving across the cat's eye. As many as six have been found in a single eye.

Your vet can remove them with forceps after administering a tranquilizer and a local anesthetic to the cat.

HEART WORMS: These parasites are more common in dogs than in cats, but our feline pets are sometimes unwilling hosts to them.

Their technical name is *Dirofilaria immitis*. The mosquito is the intermediate host. It acquires the active embryos when it sucks blood from a dog or cat, shelters the changeling worms as they grow into larvae, and then injects them back into the dog or cat in the process of sucking more blood. The embryonic worms circulate in the blood, but when the larvae get back into the body of the dog or cat, they head for the muscle and fatty tissues, there to grow until they are ready to make their way through the blood system to the heart, where they reach maturity.

The symptoms of heart-worm infection are coughing, labored breathing, and collapse when the animal exercises. A typical feline victim, cited in one of the professional journals, collapsed early one morning and was hospitalized in shock and evident pain. Its body temperature was well below normal at 97° F. The cat responded to stimulants but three hours later it collapsed again and died. An autopsy uncovered one male and four female worms in the right ventricle of the heart.

Drugs are available against heart worms. However, different drugs must be used to kill the adult worm and the embryos, called *microfilariae*. Usually the drug that kills the adult worms is administered one month before the drug designed to kill the embryos. In some cases, the vet may prefer to remove the worms surgically.

MUSCLE WORMS: Trichinosis, a parasitic disease which exists in man, is also caused in the cat by the worm called *Trichinella spiralis*. At various stages in their development, these worms inhabit almost every kind of tissue in the body. When they finally reach their destination, the muscle fibers, they encyst. The cat, like man, usually becomes infested with these worms if it eats uncooked, or undercooked, pork in which the worms are encysted.

The symptoms appear in three stages: first, for about a week there may be diarrhea, slight fever, mild abdominal pain, sometimes nausea and vomiting; second, for two or three weeks there may be loss of appetite, muscular pains, labored breathing, and low fever; third, the period of encystation, muscular stiffness, nerve disorders, lung trouble.

The best way to fight trichinosis is not to let your cat get it in the first place—not to feed it pork that hasn't been cooked long enough (thirty minutes) at a high enough temperature (212° F.). The vet can make your cat more comfortable if it becomes infested, but he can't destroy the worms without cooking the cat, which the cat might regard as a rather extreme measure.

HOOKWORMS: Three kinds of hookworm are found in the cat; their technical names are *Ancylostoma caninum, Ancylostoma braziliense,* and *Uncinaria stenocephala.*

Infested animals appear anemic and, in severe cases, produce black, tarry stools. There are sometimes respiratory difficulties.

These worms can be destroyed by biochemicals administered by your veterinarian. It is important to have him treat hookworm disease, however, because it can cause death.

ROUNDWORMS: Also called ascarids, these parasites are very common in kittens and puppies. In fact, the babies can acquire the worms while they are still in the mother cat's womb.

The symptoms include failure to grow at a normal rate, engage in normal activity, or display good condition. The coat may be dull, the body pot-bellied. There may be signs of digestive difficulties. The kitten may vomit, and the vomitus and the feces may be found on microscopic examination to harbor the roundworms.

There are a number of new drugs which are highly effective against roundworms.

TAPEWORMS: There are at least eight different cestodes or tapeworms that infest the cat. The worm segments are sometimes seen in the stool.

The symptoms include general unthriftiness, an attitude of sickness, irritability, capricious appetite, ruffled coat, colic, mild diarrhea, emaciation, and sometimes fits.

Effective drugs are available to the veterinarian for treating tapeworm infestation. A major problem, however, is the prevention of reinfestation.

This list includes only the most common worms that infest cats. It does not, by any means, exhaust the list of internal parasites to which the cat is prey. For example, there are also flukes and stomach worms.

My purpose in listing these worms was to emphasize the variety of parasites in the cat. Each of these worms is quite different from the rest; each requires a different kind of treatment. *No one but a veterinarian is competent to identify and treat the offending parasite!*

Pet shops, drugstores, and even supermarkets offer commercial "worm medicines" for sale. These patent medicines should never be used, for the following reasons:

1. A patent medicine is able to kill only one kind of worm. You may give your cat a medicine intended to kill roundworms when your cat is actually infested with hookworms. Only a vet can prescribe the right worm-killer for the right worm.

2. Many vermifuges, as worm-purge chemicals are called, must be very strong if they are to be effective. At such a strength, they can be dangerous to the cat unless their use is supervised by a vet. A commercial vermifuge, therefore, is likely to be too weak to be effective. If it is strong enough to do the job, it's dangerous to the cat's health.

3. Any vermifuge is, basically, a kind of poison. Before the cat is asked to take the shock of a worming, its general health and stamina must be assayed. For example, a cat with a heart murmur may have more difficulty withstanding a vermifuge than in carrying the extra burden of the parasites.

When a kitten is about a month old, its stool should be examined microscopically for worms by a vet. If the kitten is older when you get it, ask the vet to make such an examination the first time he sees the cat. After that, the cat should be checked from time to time when it's at the vet's office, and certainly whenever it displays any of the symptoms of worm infestation.

LEASH AND COLLAR

Some cats love to go out for walks, just as dogs do. And all cats that are confined permanently indoors like to get outdoors once in a while to enjoy the sun, the fresh air, and a nibble or two of grass. But first they must be trained to a collar (or harness) and leash. And the time for that training is when the cat is still a kitten.

Start indoors. Just put the collar or the harness on the kitten—without the leash—and then let the kitten get used to it. If it struggles to pull the collar off, try to distract its attention by playing with it.

Do this for a few minutes one day, a few more minutes the next day, and so on, gradually lengthening the time, until the kitten is accustomed to the feel of the collar about its neck.

Then attach the leash to the collar, and gradually, as with the collar, let the leash become a familiar thing to the kitten. Only when the kitten is at home with the leash and collar should you begin to guide it by gently pulling on the leash.

It takes patience—a great deal of patience—but it's worth it.

TOYS AND BONES

Cats love to play games all their lives, and they are the most remarkably inventive and imaginative of animals. Left to their own devices, they can conjure up a mouse in a rumpled bed, transform a length of string into a sinister viper, pursue a bottle cap across the floor as though it were a fleeing mouse.

There are many good toys available in pet shops. Many of them are filled with catnip, which always delights a cat (well, almost always). The toy should not have any sharp or small parts, like buttons, which the kitten could swallow, to its ultimate discomfort. Rubber balls are good—but they should be too big for the cat to swallow.

Sometimes your own ingenuity will provide the best toys. Every cat is happiest when it has a shoe box or a paper bag to climb in and out of. A crumpled-up piece of newspaper is always fun.

There are some things that cats should never be permitted to play with—pins, buttons, short lengths of string that could be swallowed and cause trouble inside the cat, rubber bands, beads, decorations, breakable glass objects, and the like. If the cat has swallowed this sort of thing and, in the case of string or stringed objects, it has been only partway eliminated, don't yield to the temptation to pull it out. There may be a hook or a knot on the string, in which case the danger of tearing delicate tissues must be considered. Let your veterinarian handle the problem.

Some cats like bones for playing and gnawing. This is quite all right, if the bones are the proper kind. The *only* bones the cat should ever be permitted to have are the large beef bones—the heavy leg bones or the big knuckle ends, whole or cut into sections. These cannot splinter in the cat's mouth. Neither can the specially processed bones sold in pet shops and pet supply sections of supermarkets.

No other bones should ever be given to your cat, regardless of whatever nonsense to the contrary you may hear or read. There are those who like to argue that a cat in the feral stage eats small rodents and fish, bones and all, so nature must protect it from the harm that bones could do. This mystical exaltation of nature is rather absurd, of course; nature doesn't protect cats from larger predators, viruses, and many other hazards. Every vet has had experience in removing bone splinters that have cut into palates or throats or stomachs. For example, the *Journal* of the American Veterinary Medical Association, in 1960, reported the case of a nine-month-old male that had become suddenly depressed, vomited, refused to eat, and had a temperature of 105° F. It was believed to be suffering from feline distemper—but an X-ray disclosed a curious chain of objects in the pharynx. Under anesthesia, the spinal column of a fish was removed from the upper part of the throat.

CAR SICKNESS

Cats, for some reason as yet not understood by science, hardly ever suffer from car sickness, unlike dogs. A cat may show abnormal fear in a car, for example by foaming, but this is not from car sickness.

7. THE ADULT CAT

Not as a bond-servant or dependent has this proudest of mammals entered the human fraternity; not as a slave like the beasts of burden, or a humble camp follower like the dog. The cat is domestic only as far as suits its own ends; it will not be kenneled or harnessed nor suffer any dictation as to its goings-out or comings-in.

—SAKI (Hector Hugh Munro) (1870-1916)

IN 1607 Edward Topsell, the early English zoologist, offered his advice on how to keep a house cat. "Those which will keep their cats within doors, and from hunting birds abroad," he wrote, "must cut off their ears, for they cannot endure to have drops of rain distill into them, and therefore keep themselves in harbor."

This drastic method for curbing the cat's wanderlust has, happily, gone out of fashion since Topsell's day. Nowadays the question is not: Indoors or out? It is, rather: City or country?

It is true, of course, that cats, unlike dogs, are not required to be licensed in most communities (although a few places, such as Saddle Brook, New Jersey, have ordinances that force cats to be licensed and belled). Thus a city pet can legally be permitted to roam at will.

Some city dwellers prefer to give their cats the freedom of the streets rather than keep sanitary pans for them indoors. I once had a neighbor who lived in a first-floor apartment. She kept a length of carpeting hanging out a rear window. Her cat would climb down on the carpet until it could drop to the ground. Then it would go about its business. When it was ready to return home, the cat would leap up, catch hold of the carpeting, and climb up in through the window.

Usually city pets are kept indoors all the time. The cats that roam free have a much shorter life expectancy because of automobile traffic, poison, cat stealers, feline plagues, and infections from rodents.

In the suburbs, it's often a toss-up whether a cat should be kept indoors or permitted to roam. Uncastrated males must be permitted out because of their objectionable scent. But many people like to let their cats enjoy the sport of hunting. To make matters more convenient for the cat's master, a tiny cat's door can be cut into the back door so the cat can go in and out at will. A ready-made cat's door for this purpose is on the market now.

In addition to the city hazards, however, suburban and country cats face the danger of being hunted by cat-haters. Cat owners usually are unaware that the cat does not enjoy the kind of legal protection that guards the dog against trigger-happy hunters. Almost every state has a provision like this. In New York, for example, the state conservation law, Section 205, reads:

> Any person over the age of twenty-one years possessing a hunting license may, and game protectors and other peace officers shall, humanely destroy cats at large found hunting or killing any bird protected by law, or with a dead bird of any species protected by law in its possession, and no action for damages shall lie for such killing.

This is an absurd and unfair law. Who is to say whether a cat creeping along the ground is hunting a "bird protected by law" or a mouse? If a cat comes upon a dead bird lying on the ground and stops to sniff at it, is the bird then to be presumed "in its possession?" In effect, this law provides for an open season on cats the year 'round.

This attitude has been upheld by the Supreme Court of Oklahoma, which exonerated a chicken breeder who had killed a cat outside his backyard. But in Canada the courts have held that—although there may be some circumstances under which a cat may properly be killed —it is not justifiable to kill the cat simply because it is trespassing on one's property, even if it is hunting game.

Such legal discrimination against cats also is evident in the larceny statutes. In most states the law classes the stealing of a dog as larceny, but makes no mention of the theft of a cat. In the common law, however, any pet is a thing of value and its theft is therefore larceny.

But cats deserve much more protection from the law—at least as much protection as dogs—for cats are collected for use in laboratory experiments on an even greater scale than dogs. Indeed, the traffic in dogs and cats for laboratories is on a scale undreamed-of by most people.

In 1960 a Wisconsin company sent out an announcement to Midwestern high school students. The announcement, addressed to "any groups or classes of high school students wishing to raise money now," offered fifty cents each for "all the cats you can collect for cash." The company planned to kill the cats, embalm them, and send them to school laboratories. "You will be surprised just how easy it is to collect 150-300 cats," said the announcement. The company was surprised, almost immediately, by the protests from cat lovers who had been alerted by *Cats Magazine*. In the face of this reaction, the company withdrew its offer, but not before "some schools had collected and sold us cats," as a company spokesman conceded.

OTHER LEGAL CONSIDERATIONS

Is a cat owner responsible for the acts of his pet? Does he have any recourse in law if another person, or an animal belonging to another person, does injury to the cat?

These are questions which occasionally puzzle cat owners. It is important that they be aware of their responsibilities and rights.

The courts generally recognize the propensities of the cat. Let us assume that your cat invades your neighbor's house, sees a parrot sitting on its perch, pounces upon it, kills it, and carries it off. This sort of thing is likely to strain relations between you and your neighbor— or, at the very least, to moderate your neighbor's enthusiasm for your cat—but such a misfortune will not subject you to a lawsuit. A Pennsylvania court and a British appellate court have both held that cats cannot be kept under the same restraint and discipline as dogs, and therefore their owners cannot be held responsible for their acts while roaming.

On the other hand, if your neighbor should catch the cat trespassing and kill it, there's nothing much you can do about that. The cat's depredations, in that case, have made it fair prey.

Cat bites and scratches can be another problem. There is, for example, the case of the woman who is bitten and clawed by a household pet. She may, or may not, recover damages from the cat's owner. In such a case, a Connecticut court has held, the victim must prove that the cat was known to be vicious and aggressive, and that the cat's owner, knowing this, did nothing to restrain the cat. But if the cat is just an ordinary cat, with no special delight in attacking humans, or if the owner had no reason to believe otherwise, then the victim cannot hope to win a damage suit.

In Massachusetts, a woman who owned a dog broke up a fight it was having with a cat. After the animals had been separated, the woman took the cat's paw in her hand, and promptly got herself bitten and scratched, as any cat owner might have predicted. The court held that the woman had been negligent, even though she'd grabbed the cat's paw because she was afraid the cat might go at the dog again.

If a cat is wrongfully injured by a person or an animal belonging to another person, the cat's owner has the right to recover damages, provided that the injury was the result of a willful act or of negligence on the part of the person. If the cat's owner has been guilty of contributory negligence, however, the right to recovery does not apply.

HUNTING AND TROPHIES

As the courts have recognized, hunting is basic to a cat's nature. The cat doesn't hunt because it is hungry, although many people mistakenly think so. (It is a pity how many cats are starved because humans think the animals will hunt better in that condition.) There is even a good deal of evidence that a hungry cat isn't as good a hunter as a well-fed cat: its reflexes aren't as fast, its sight may be impaired by malnutrition, its strength is sapped by the lack of nourishment. The sleek cat with the contented stomach is in much better shape to use all its patience, wit, agility, and strength in the hunt.

In ancient Egypt, cats were trained to hunt as retrievers, even recovering game from the water, for some cats—not many—enjoy swimming. Today I know of no cats that hunt with their masters.

As a solitary hunter, however, the cat is well-nigh unbeatable. Its killing of birds, rabbits, rats, mice, shrews, and snakes helps to maintain the balance of nature. There is even reason to believe that the cat is all that stands between man and the plague. The cat should not be discouraged by a squeamish owner from the pursuit of its natural prey. It is merely fulfilling its role in nature's great cycle. Besides, the cat owner must be realistic about his own limitations; nothing he can do will make the cat change its favorable attitude toward hunting. My declawed cat, who happens to be deaf, killed a mouse in an apartment once—how, I don't know, for there was no mark of violence on the poor little creature.

One of the most distressing aspects of the cat's hunting instinct is the cat's pride. Many cats insist on bringing their dead prey home as trophies to be presented proudly to their humans. This is sometimes a little too much for humans to stomach. A white cat of my acquaintance used to bring home at least one trophy—usually a rat or a field mouse, but occasionally a rabbit, squirrel, or bird—every day. One day, while the mistress of the house was having a cocktail party, the cat slipped into the house through an open window, trophy in mouth, and proceeded to put it down on the floor beside the hors d'oeuvres table. It created quite a stir.

BIRDS

The cat is fascinated by birds and will stalk its feathered prey whenever it can. Nevertheless, it is possible to keep both cats and birds. At Animal Talent Scouts, in Manhattan, I've seen birds walking unconcernedly along the floor in front of cats who couldn't have been more disinterested. To achieve this state of affairs requires constant vigilance, a suspicious mind (as to the cat's motives at any given moment), and the ability to discipline a cat. With sufficient discipline, the cat can be made to learn that the bird is not to be considered food for more than thought.

For this sort of discipline, a water pistol is very useful. Keep the pistol filled and sit within range of the birdcage. Every time the cat approaches the cage or shows an interest in the bird, shoot some water at the cat. It's remarkable how chastened a cat can become when hit suddenly by a jet of water out of nowhere.

Bird lovers usually assume that cats outdoors spend all their time hunting birds. This is demonstrable error. At least two studies have been made, in Wisconsin and Oklahoma, of the stomach contents of cats killed while roving. In Wisconsin, of fifty cats examined, seven had been pets, thirty-nine had been hunters without established abodes, and two had been feral. In Oklahoma all of the cats subjected to post-mortem examination were feral.

The Wisconsin cats' last meals were classed like this: meadow mice, twenty-six cats; deer mice, eight cats; house mice, three cats; unidentified mice, nine cats; Norway rats, seven cats; rabbits, three cats; short-tailed shrew, one cat; chicken heads and feet (apparently stolen from human garbage), three cats; grasshoppers, three cats; crickets, one cat; June bugs, one cat; human food remnants, twenty-one cats. One cat had swallowed a heavy cord and another a piece of cloth. Only six of the fifty cats had fed on birds. Of these birds, three were unidentified small birds, two were English sparrows, and one was a pigeon.

The Oklahoma cats had similar tastes. Fifty-five percent had eaten rodents; 12½ percent, insects; 2 percent, reptiles; 26½ percent, human food. Only 4 percent had enjoyed a bird as the last meal.

Obviously, cats kill fewer birds than hunters do in duck and pheasant season. Moreover, a few cats each year are killed by birds, usually by the great horned owl, although eagles also carry off cats. (The cat is also prey to the dog, the fox, the coyote, and the lynx.) Nevertheless, bird lovers from time to time raise a great hue and cry about cats. In a few communities they have even succeeded in enacting laws requiring that all cats be collared, belled, and leashed.

When Adlai E. Stevenson was Governor of Illinois, the Legislature of that state passed a cat control measure. The Governor vetoed the bill. His veto message has become a classic:

> I cannot agree that it should be the declared public policy of
> Illinois that a cat visiting a neighbor's yard or crossing the highway

is a public nuisance. It is the nature of cats to do a certain amount of unescorted roaming. Many live with their owners in apartments or other restricted premises, and I doubt if we want to make their every brief foray an opportunity for a small game hunt by zealous citizens—with traps or otherwise.

I am afraid this bill could only create discord, recrimination, and enmity.

Also consider the owner's dilemma: To escort a cat abroad on a leash is against the nature of a cat, and to permit it to venture forth for exercise unattended into a night of new dangers is against the nature of the owner.

Moreover, cats perform useful service, particularly in rural areas, in combatting rodents—work they necessarily perform alone and without regard for property lines.

We are all interested in protecting certain varieties of bird. That cats destroy some birds, I well know, but I believe this legislation would further but little the worthy cause to which its proponents give such unselfish effort. The problem of cat versus bird is as old as time. If we attempt to resolve it by legislation, who knows but what we may be called upon to take sides as well in the age-old problems of dog versus cat, bird versus bird, or even bird versus worm.

In my opinion, the State of Illinois and its local governing bodies already have enough to do without trying to control feline delinquency.

CAT FIGHTS

There are few things in this world so noisy, wild, fierce, and thoroughly frightful as an out-and-out cat fight—as distinguished from a cat skirmish of the sort that occurs frequently without any serious results. Most cat fights are between unaltered adult males or between a whole cat and a neutered cat.

The owner's impulse is to plunge into the fray and separate the two cats, but this is most unwise. The two animals are so excited that they are virtually incapable of recognizing a human identity. Every fiber of their bodies is keyed to the fight. They will lash out at anything that hinders their attempts to defend themselves and attack their foes. In this momentary kind of madness, the cat will even unwittingly attack its own master. The human who tries to separate two fighting cats, therefore, is almost certain to be badly bitten and clawed for his trouble.

There are two ways to separate fighting cats. The first is to throw water on them. A bucket of water flung on a couple of fighting cats has an immediate, sobering effect on them.

The other method is to fling a heavy blanket or some other kind of cloth over the cats. Once they are entangled in the folds they will tend to separate of their own accord.

Regardless of which method is employed, the cat owner should be careful not to pick up his cat immediately after the fight, because the cat is still likely to strike out instinctively. It is better to wait a few moments, murmuring comfortingly to the cat until it shows that it has calmed down enough to be handled.

HABITS—GOOD AND BAD

Whatever your own politics may be, there is one fact of life that you'd better be prepared to admit to yourself: the cat is a confirmed conservative. It is even a diehard.

The cat demands an ordered existence. Except in its sex life, the cat is no Bohemian. It likes to have its meals at the same time and place every day. It likes to have the same place to sleep. It likes to have furniture in the same place every day. You may, if you wish, live your own carefree, helter-skelter life, but one day the cat will pack its things and go off to find some humans who know that calendars and clocks and decorators' schemes are not to be trifled with.

Without training, the cat will learn to recognize the sound of your footstep or your car, and you'll find the cat waiting for you whenever you return home. The cat also has a time sense, and it will know, and expect, a break in routine on weekends.

But there are other habits that require training. If you want to keep the cat off the tables or other furniture, you can train it to respect those areas. But it's not easily done. It's long-drawn-out and often discouraging. You must keep after the cat constantly when it tries the forbidden.

Often a cat will develop a taste for your house plants. The best thing to do if that happens is to put the plants in a room from which the cat can be barred. A taste for house plants can be dangerous for the cat. Some plants can be poisonous to it. A Brooklyn veterinarian, Dr. Bernard Wasserman, in a report published in the *Journal* of the American Veterinary Medical Association, described a cat that died after eating the leaves of a house plant later identified as sheep laurel, *Kalmia angustifolia*.

Some cats develop a habit of chewing electrical cords. This problem is described in the next chapter, pages 145 and 146.

Sometimes a cat's bad habits are created by its owner. A cat that scratches in playing usually does so because its owner started out playing the teasing game of wiggling his finger in front of the cat and then snatching it away. The cat, not unnaturally, grabs with its claws in an effort to catch the finger. This sort of game should be played with a piece of string or a pencil, not with your finger. There is no reason why a cat owner's hand should be constantly scratched.

TRICKS

It is generally believed that cats cannot be taught to do tricks. That is not true. It is true, however, that cats are far more difficult to teach than dogs—not because they are less intelligent, but because they are too sensible to think that sort of thing is really worthwhile.

Therefore, to teach a cat tricks you must make it worth the cat's while. If you want the cat to come on call, call it when it is close to you and immediately give it a treat as a reward. Do this a few times and the cat will soon realize that when you call its name there's a treat worth coming for. The same can be done with whistling.

If the cat does what you want it to do, exactly right, praise it and reward it. If it is not quite right, say, "No, No," and make it do the trick again. Reward the cat only when it has done the trick perfectly. And praise it over and over again.

Train the cat for only about five minutes at a time, with a rest of at least a half hour between training sessions. Never train the cat if its attention is wandering to other things.

If owners are patient enough, cats can be taught to shake hands, lie down and roll over, come on command, stay indoors, jump through a hoop, retrieve, talk, sit up and beg, sit in a designated place, and wave goodbye.

GROOMING

The comb and brush to be used in grooming the cat have been discussed in Chapter 3. A somewhat unorthodox addition to that equipment is your vacuum cleaner. Most cats love to be vacuumed; their exhibition of pleasure is nothing less than orgiastic. It's an unusual way to rid the cat of dead hair.

Whether the cat is long-haired or short-haired, it should be brushed frequently—if possible, every day. This need is particularly urgent in the case of long-haired cats, as one might expect. The long-hair's coat should be brushed and combed carefully down to the skin, and any mats should be eliminated. If this is neglected, the time will come when the cat will be forced to endure a rather painful and unhappy session with a brush.

A mat is a mass of hairs stuck together as though with glue. It is most often found on the underside or on the back legs of long-hairs. A twig, a thistle, a piece of leaf may be the initial factor in the development of the mat.

A long-hair's coat should first be brushed against the normal lie of the hair, and later in the direction that the coat lies. The brush should be worked against the coat in short, controlled strokes, taking a very small section of coat at a time.

As hair collects in the brush and comb, clean them up and then resume brushing and combing. The comb is used after the brushing has been completed.

If no amount of brushing removes a mat, it may be possible to break it up by moistening it to soften it, then breaking it up with the blunt —*not* the sharp—end of a knitting needle. In unusually stubborn cases, which are almost always the result of neglect on the part of the owner, it may be necessary to cut the mat out with scissors.

Short-haired cats present much less of a problem in grooming. The brushing and combing is quite simple. A hound's glove, available in most pet shops, is sometimes a handy additional tool.

When the grooming of a long-haired cat has been completed, you may still have reason to believe that there is dirt in the coat. If that is so, don't bathe the cat. Instead, have your pet dealer or veterinarian recommend a safe dry bath powder for the cat. Apply the powder as directed by the label, being careful to remove all the powder afterward.

FLEAS, TICKS, LICE

When you are grooming the cat, you should also keep your eyes open for any signs of certain external parasites, such as fleas, ticks, and lice. These minute creatures can cause discomfort, suffering, crippling, and even death.

FLEAS: Some cats never catch fleas, but most cats do. Why some are apparently immune is still a matter for speculation.

There are several varieties of flea which afflict the cat. These fleas will also trouble humans if there are no cats about. And they like dogs about as well as cats. The cat flea, *Ctenocephalides felis,* is more common than the dog flea, *Ctenocephalides canis,* although their indiscriminate habits make the names of both these fleas somewhat misleading.

The flea is a small, wingless (it hops), blood-sucking parasite. Its eggs develop on the ground, in the cat's bedding, or in crevices in the floor, so that even while you're getting rid of the fleas on your cat, new fleas may be maturing in contact with the cat.

For this reason, many persons prefer a remedial powder instead of the sprays and baths made for this purpose. The cat will shake powder to the floor and into its bed, and thus kill many of the developing fleas as well as those already on its body.

No powder, spray, or bath using DDT, Rothane (TDE), lindane, benzene hexachloride (BHC), toxaphene, or malathion should ever be applied to a cat. These are all highly poisonous to cats.

On the cat, fleas will be found most often around the head, the ears, the back of the neck, the rump, and the tail.

Often the flea bites will have set up a serious skin irritation. It is best to let your veterinarian manage the treatment of this condition. There are a number of soothing treatments that he can apply.

TICKS: Until recently, ticks were mostly found in the Midwestern, Western, and Southern states. In the past decade they have extended their territory to cover almost all of our country. They are exasperating, pernicious, and persistent pests. They can be dangerous to cat, dog, and man.

There are many varieties of this blood-sucking insect, and unfortunately all of them are perfectly happy to make a home on a cat.

The tick has a fearsome mouth and jaws, and with these it bites deeply into the skin of its host, so deeply that almost all of its head may be buried in the cat's skin as the tick's belly swells with the blood it is sucking. If you succumb to temptation and tug at the tick, all you'll get is the body. The head and jaws will remain buried in the cat, to fester and cause a serious infection.

The correct way to remove a tick is to soak a small piece of cotton or a Q-Tip in ether or alcohol and then press it against the insect until it releases its grip and can be lifted away intact. But the tick is still not dead. The best way to dispose of it, after it has been removed from the cat, is to burn it.

In massive infestations of ticks, your veterinarian may prefer to give the cat a tick dip. This is all right for the vet, but you should not attempt it, for the cat is susceptible to poisoning by some of the substances commonly used in animal dips.

LICE: There are two types of lice, the biters and the bloodsuckers. It is the biter that usually attacks the cat.

Lice can kill a cat rather quickly. Moreover, lice on a mother cat will quickly migrate from her to her kittens, and will almost surely kill them.

Even when the lice are killed, the nits (louse eggs) remain on the hair as a continuing menace. This is, clearly, a parasite difficult to destroy.

If you suspect the presence of lice on your cat—frequent scratching should attract your attention to the cat's problem—the best thing to do is to take the cat to the vet and let him prescribe the chemical to be used and the method of treatment.

HAIR BALLS

Regular grooming will help to cut down on the development of hair balls, a curious phenomenon in the cat.

Hair balls result from the cat's habit of licking its coat frequently every day. This hair collects in the stomach. From time to time, perhaps a month or two apart, the cat regurgitates the hair in a cylindrical, feltlike roll.

If the hair ball escapes from the stomach into the intestine, the pylorus (the exit valve from the stomach) prevents the cat from vomiting the hair ball. Then the cat is in trouble. The cat stops eating. At this point the cat should be taken to a veterinarian. Surgery may be necessary.

Preparations are available in pet shops for encouraging the elimination of hair balls. These products usually consist of petroleum jelly flavored to be especially palatable to the cat. The jelly is applied to the cat's nose, and the animal promptly licks it off. In the cat's stomach, the jelly acts as a lubricant.

The same use can be made of plain petroleum jelly, although the cat won't like it as well. However, mineral oil, which is sometimes recommended for this purpose, should be used only with the greatest caution. If mineral oil is not properly dropped into the cat's mouth, it may go into the windpipe and ultimately the lungs, instead of the esophagus and then the stomach.

The natural function of the hair ball has been a matter for speculation. Hawks and owls, it has been pointed out, disgorge the indigestible parts of their prey in pellets with bones inside and fur and feathers outside. When cats are permitted to roam and hunt freely, Dr. W. R. McCuistion argues, their hair balls often are found to contain small animal teeth, claws, beaks, bones, scales, burrs, and other rough material. Is the purpose of the hair ball to protect the cat's insides from the sharp bits of material it swallows and then must regurgitate?

TRAVELING

Although they rarely suffer from motion sickness, most cats are not good travelers. Occasionally one will meet a cat that loves to ride in a car, but such a cat is the exception, not the rule. Most cats are much too conservative to enjoy being uprooted and carted off on some uncomfortable journey to a place that's really not better than home. So if you *must* travel with a cat, take precautions. A cat loose in a car is likely to get frightened easily, and it's quite a feat to drive a car while trying to capture and pacify a cat that's climbing about one's head. To avoid this predicament, make sure the cat is in a carrying case. You can open the case a little from time to time, of course, to pet the cat, and it will hear the soothing sounds of your voice even when the case is closed. If the case fastens with a bolt and hasp, it's best to use a padlock instead of the bolt for your journey, because cats can be devilishly clever at opening supposedly secure cages and cases.

If you're traveling by car, you must remember the cat's sanitary requirements. If you're going by train or plane, you'll probably be permitted to keep the case with you at your seat.

Since cats don't enjoy traveling, it may be well to ask your veterinarian for a tranquilizer to give to the cat before starting out.

Your vet is also the best source of information about boarding facilities if you must travel but cannot take your cat—or do not want to. Follow the vet's advice in this, for boarding facilities can be reservoirs of disease, and your vet is best equipped to know which places are the safest.

MOVING

It follows that a cat, which doesn't enjoy travel, will not enjoy moving to a new house. This problem is easily handled, however.

THE ADULT CAT

Put the cat in its carrying case before the movers begin taking the furniture out of the house. Then release the cat in the new house in one closed room which contains some furniture to which the cat is accustomed. After the rest of the furniture is moved in, the cat can be led out to wander through the rest of the house, exploring. If the cat continues to show distress in its new home, try smearing butter on its paws and legs. The cat will be so distracted by its need to lick them clean of the awful stuff that it will forget all about its unhappiness over the move.

8. FIRST AID AND HEALTH CARE

BEFORE you begin ordering the cat to stick out its tongue and say, "Ahhhh!" let me explain that it is not the intention or function of this book to transform the cat owner into a Doctor of Veterinary Medicine. Nor into a hypochondriac.

In this chapter, however, you will find information on home nursing of the sick cat, what to do in emergencies, and—most important of all—the symptoms that warn you of serious illness that requires the professional attention of a veterinarian.

The cat is subject to a remarkable range of serious illnesses, and disease usually rages within the cat's body for some time before it is detected. Unlike illness in man, diagnosis is frustrated for the cat by the animal's inability to express its pain or discomfort in plain words. But the cat does communicate to the observant cat owner, and in this chapter you will learn how to interpret the feline language of health and sickness.

Moreover, the cat, because of its curiosity, agility, and courage, has the knack of getting into more difficulties than anyone but an overworked humane society rescue worker could ever imagine. So you

136

must learn how to take care of the cat after accidents and odd—that's just the word for them—and assorted mishaps.

FIRST-AID SUPPLIES

Before trouble strikes, the prudent cat owner will lay in those supplies which are most likely to be needed in an emergency. Some of these are supplies which one might keep on hand for the humans in the family, but a few may be unexpected. The cat's first-aid kit should include the following:

A RECTAL THERMOMETER: this can be either a rectal thermometer intended for veterinary use or one intended for measuring human temperatures. It really doesn't matter.

ASPIRIN: these tablets should be the "baby" aspirin, available at any pharmacy. Each tablet provides 1¼ grains of aspirin, which makes each pill one-fourth the strength of the five-grain tablet usually taken by adult humans. Eases pain, reduces temperature.

MILK OF MAGNESIA: liquid or tablets. A laxative.

KAOPECTATE: a liquid preparation that helps in the control of diarrhea.

PEROXIDE: the 3 percent solution which is a drugstore standard. Useful as an antiseptic and for inducing vomiting.

GAUZE BANDAGE ROLLS: the two- or three-inch standard rolls are just right for making bandage pads, compresses, bandages, and tourniquets.

STERILE COTTON: besides its frequent use as a cushioning element under bandages, this is also handy for removing ticks, cleaning ears, and many other uses.

ADHESIVE TAPE.

RUBBING ALCOHOL: for removing ticks, cleaning the thermometer, etc.

VASELINE: for lubricating thermometer before inserting it into the cat's rectum. (Be careful that the petrolatum you use is not carbolated, for that can poison a cat.)

YELLOW MERCURIC OXIDE OPHTHALMIC OINTMENT: to relieve

minor eye irritations and to protect the eyes when soap or chemicals must be applied near the eyes.

UNIVERSAL ANTIDOTE: for use if the cat has been poisoned. This is discussed in detail in the section on poisoning later in this chapter.

No medication containing phenol (carbolic acid) should be administered to a cat. It is believed to be toxic to cats.

TEMPERATURE

The normal body temperature of the adult cat averages 101.5 degrees Fahrenheit, but a degree below or above that is within the normal range. (If you have a centigrade thermometer, the equivalent temperature is 38.6 degrees.)

If the cat's temperature is not normal, don't panic. Many factors besides illness can affect temperature. These factors include age, sex, season, time of day, environmental temperature, exercise, eating, digestion, and drinking of water. Kittens usually run temperatures about a degree higher than adult cats. The difference is even greater in diseased cats: a kitten with an infection may have a very high temperature, but an old cat's temperature may be normal, or close to normal, even when it is seriously diseased.

Cats love heat and sunlight, and on a hot summer day a cat may stretch out in the sun for a snooze. For this reason, many cat owners underestimate the effect of environmental temperatures on the cat. Cats *do* become overheated on occasion. Scientists have found that 90 degrees is the critical temperature. When the temperature of the surrounding air hits 90 degrees, the temperature of the cat's body begins to go up. Before the body temperature rises, the rate of breathing increases and the cat begins to pant. Panting is a cooling device—it causes the increased evaporation of water from the tongue and mouth. When it is hot the cat will appear to clean its coat much more often than it usually does. Actually, the cat, in a wonderful instinctive response, is spreading saliva on its coat; the evaporation of the saliva adds its bit to the general body effort to lower the temperature. In very hot weather, as a matter of fact, the salivary flow in the cat is greater than it is at more comfortable temperatures.

Heat becomes dangerous to the cat when the temperature of the air hits 105° F. and the relative humidity rises above 65 percent. If those conditions persist for any length of time, the cat is likely to collapse with heat exhaustion. It can die. (See p. 143.)

Clearly, the cat's temperature is an extremely important indicator of its general well-being. Whenever you have reason to believe that the cat is sick, you should take its temperature before telephoning the veterinarian, unless the cat is so excited that you cannot manage to do the job. With most cats, it's no great difficulty to take its temperature single-handedly. Plump the cat down on your lap, coat the bulb end of the thermometer with Vaseline, and insert it about half an inch into the cat's rectum. The thermometer should be kept in the cat for three minutes. If the cat is on your lap, you can keep it under restraint by pressing your left arm along its body, keeping its head in the crook of your left elbow, and murmuring soothingly to it all the time. Your right hand will be occupied in keeping the thermometer inside the cat.

HOW TO RESTRAIN A CAT

Because of its incomparable natural endowments, a cat seems to have the strength of ten animals—especially if you're trying to restrain it. But there are many circumstances in which it is necessary to restrain the cat in order to help it.

There are three problem areas to be controlled: the forelegs, the hindlegs, and the teeth. Many an unfortunate cat owner—or veterinarian—has restrained the legs but forgotten the teeth, to his subsequent regret.

The method of restraint depends on the area of the cat's body that must be treated. If you want to apply medicine, say, to any part of the cat's head or neck, wrap the rest of its body in a thick towel, or tuck it into a laundry bag with only the cat's head out of the bag.

If the area to be treated is elsewhere on the body, two persons are needed to restrain the cat. One holds the cat's head with one hand and its forelegs with the other hand, the other person holds the hindlegs and administers the medication.

Remember that a sick or injured cat is governed to a very large extent by its instincts, rather than its conscious mind. The most gentle of cats may very well scratch or bite its beloved master or mistress when it is handled at such times. Accept this fact and conduct yourself accordingly, and both you and the cat will profit in the end.

GIVING MEDICINE

It's not at all difficult to give a cat medicine in pill or liquid form—once you get the hang of it.

Every effort should be made to get pills down the throat, and not merely into the mouth. If the pill is in the mouth, the cat may bite into it, and the medication often tastes bitter or even nauseating. To administer a pill, sit the cat on your lap or on a table, facing your right. Take the cat's entire head in your left hand, with the middle finger against one corner of the cat's mouth and the thumb against the other corner. Tip the cat's head back until its nose points to the ceiling. With the pill in your right hand, *gently* force the cat's lower jaw down with that hand, while exerting pressure on both corners of the mouth with the fingers of your left hand, thus opening the mouth. Drop the pill at the back of the tongue, where it touches the palate, and close the mouth.

Liquid medication requires a plastic beak-tipped medicine dropper. Don't use a glass dropper—it could break in the cat's mouth.

Great care must be taken in administering liquid medicine to a cat. If the liquid goes down the windpipe instead of the esophagus, there may be serious consequences.

The best way to give liquid medicine to a cat is the lip-pocket method. The preparation for this is the same as that described above for pills, except that the head is not tilted back. With the head level, take the loose skin at one corner of the mouth—where the upper and lower jaws meet—and lift it away from the teeth. You will find that this forms a loose sort of pouch. Empty the medicine dropper's contents into the pouch and then let the skin go back to its natural position, but hold the cat's mouth shut for a moment.

It has happened on rare occasions that a medicine dropper falls into the cat's mouth in the midst of these exertions. If it does, turn the cat upside down immediately, with its hindquarters up in the air and its head hanging down, and shake it vigorously. The medicine dropper usually will drop out at once.

BANDAGES

Rare is the cat owner who can apply a bandage that will remain in place on the cat. Veterinarians are able to perform minor miracles of bandaging, however. My own vet applies a bandage so skillfully that the cat isn't troubled by it at all, but cleans it in the firm conviction that the bandage is a part of its coat.

If the cat fusses about a bandage, however, try smearing some butter on the cat's legs. The cat will be so busy cleaning the butter from its coat that it will forget all about the hated bandage.

ACCIDENTS

When a mishap of some kind has befallen your cat—and cats are able to have some remarkably unlikely accidents—it's up to you to keep calm and use your wits. If you panic, if you fail to think clearly, you will fail your pet when it needs you most. Don't try to do everything at once. Take the time to think out what you're going to do. The few seconds you spend on thinking about the problem cannot conceivably cost the cat its life, but they might save it.

Keep the cat as quiet as possible. It should be kept lying down, if necessary under restraint.

Check for wounds and bleeding. If there is a heavy flow of blood from a wound, apply a pressure bandage—a heavy pad of absorbent material covered with gauze or other cloth and held in place by adhesive tape. It may be unconventional, but a sanitary napkin of the type manufactured for women is ideal for this purpose.

If there is no profuse external bleeding, examine the cat's gums. If they are white or very light pink, there's a possibility that the cat is bleeding internally.

Keep the cat as warm as possible. It should have a blanket or heavy towel under it and another over it. Lift the cat as little as possible; in fact, any movement of the cat is undesirable.

Call the vet and *calmly* describe to him the accident, the apparent injuries, and the cat's overall appearance. Omit nothing; the vet isn't a mind-reader.

Usually the vet will ask you to bring the cat to his office. If so, you must move the cat as quietly and carefully as possible. Wrap a blanket, towel, or coat around the cat to immobilize it and keep it warm, slip one hand under the cat's head and neck and the other under its hindquarters. As you lift the cat, try to keep it level.

SHOCK

One of the most baffling and dangerous of all physiological phenomena is shock. Scientists still do not understand its cause and function. Shock occurs after, and as a result of, serious stress, such as serious accidents, heart trouble, massive hemorrhage, burns, overwhelming infections, blockage of the alimentary tract, anemia, dehydration, poisoning, and electrical contact. (See p. 146 for treating electrical shock.)

Shock can be fatal, so it is important to know its symptoms: a lack of interest in everything, prostration, a lowered temperature, shallow and rapid breathing, thirst, vomiting, and diarrhea.

Keep the cat warm. Stroke it and act as reassuringly as possible toward it.

But these are only first-aid measures. In any serious case of shock, the services of a veterinarian are needed urgently. He can take vigorous steps to counteract the shock, including blood transfusions, corticosteroid injections, and oxygen therapy.

HEAT STROKE

Extremely high air temperature, high relative humidity, and inadequate ventilation are the usual causes of heat stroke. As indicated above in the section on temperature, a cat cannot long withstand a temperature of 105 degrees Fahrenheit and relative humidity over 65 percent.

When heat stroke occurs, it is quite sudden. There is very little time to act if the cat's life is to be saved. The cat's breathing abruptly becomes deep and rapid, like that of a long-distance runner gulping air after a race. The cat collapses. There is often a staring expression in the eyes. Sometimes there is vomiting. The body temperature soars as high as 110° F.

First aid must be applied as quickly as possible. The aim is to bring down the cat's temperature. Immersion in cold water or application of liberal amounts of cold water to the body of the cat is recommended. Ice packs applied to the head are helpful, too.

It's wise to check the cat's temperature with the rectal thermometer every five minutes, because it is undesirable to bring the temperature down too fast.

CUTS

Broken glass, tacks, nails, barbed wire, jagged metal edges on cans, and many other hazards can cause serious cuts. Usually the cuts are not lethal.

First aid for cuts requires trimming of the hair around the cut. This is especially important when the injured cat is a long-hair.

Then the cut should be cleaned gently. A mild soap and water lather can be used or, better still, the germicidal soap, pHisoHex, available in all pharmacies. It is well to follow with a second cleansing, this time using peroxide solution. Be sure to dry the cut thoroughly with a sterile material after cleansing.

An extensive cut should be painted with Isodine and covered with a bandage, and then the cat should be taken to the veterinarian, so that the wound can be sutured. A deep cut can be adequately cleaned out only by the vet.

If a cut in the foot bleeds excessively—and this is not uncommon—it may be necessary to apply a tourniquet. A handkerchief will do. Tie it loosely around the leg, either above or below the ankle, and tighten it by twisting a pencil between loop and leg. Release the pressure briefly every five or ten minutes.

BITES

First aid for bites is essentially the same as for cuts. It is even more important, however, that the cat receive the prompt attention of a veterinarian, for the puncture wounds inflicted by other cats, dogs, rats, squirrels, and the like often are deep. If the wound is not thoroughly cleansed in its entire depth, abscesses are likely to develop.

The possibility of serious infection is greater in bites than in cuts, of course. Even if the animal that bit your cat is not rabid (rabies will be discussed later in this chapter), it may very well be carrying dangerous germs in its mouth.

Puncture wounds of the type inflicted by fangs often close up so completely that they pass unnoticed by the cat's owner. Your first indication that something is wrong may be the swelling that signifies the presence of an abscess. This means that the skin has healed over the wound, sealing it off from the air and trapping the germs inside. The veterinarian can open the abscess, clean it out, and treat the cat with antibiotics and other medications.

Rodent ulcers are often assumed to be caused by rat bites; hence their name. In fact, no one really knows what causes these nasty lesions. The first appearance is on the lip, where a thickened, protruding ulcer appears, sometimes in association with eczema. Some veterinarians suspect that the ulcer may originate in an allergic condition, which is then irritated by the rough surface of the cat's tongue. Other lesions appear elsewhere in and around the mouth and often the sores are spread, apparently by licking, to other parts of the body, such as the inner surface of the thigh. Some rodent ulcers become malignant, and must be removed surgically. Your veterinarian can treat most other rodent ulcers with gentian violet, protective ointments, radiation, or injection of ACTH and related drugs into the abdominal cavity. But be patient with the vet's efforts, for rodent ulcers are unpredictable in their response to medication, and only trial and error will disclose the best treatment for your particular cat.

144

FIRST AID AND HEALTH CARE

DROWNING

Not all cats hate immersion in water, although all cats do hate to get just their paws wet. There are cats that enjoy swimming. And there are other cats that fall into water accidentally. Sometimes a cat may nearly drown before it can be fished out of the water. That calls for artificial respiration.

Hold the cat up by its hindlegs and let the water drain out of its mouth. Then put the cat on the ground and sit beside it. Make sure that the cat's tongue is pulled to the side of the mouth. Then begin the alternating imposition and relaxation of pressure on the cat's chest.

Put your whole hand on the cat's side behind the shoulder, press firmly but gently (don't break the rib cage), then let up. Press again, let up. Press again, let up. Press for two or three seconds, let up for two or three seconds, press for two or three seconds—and maintain that rhythm as long as there is a heartbeat. In most cases the cat will respond after ten or twenty minutes and begin to breathe again by itself, shallowly at first, then with increasing depth and strength.

When the cat is breathing by itself, keep it warm and quiet, for it is almost certain to be suffering from some degree of shock as a result of its experience.

ELECTRIC SHOCK

When a cat suffers electric shock, it is usually because it has chewed through an electric cord. Some cats insist on chewing electric cords. Covering the cord with cayenne pepper or some other substance that the cat hates may help; on the other hand, you may merely give your cat a taste for cayenne pepper. There are also commercial preparations available in pet shops which are supposed to make cats avoid cords; these are effective with some cats. If nothing else works, you can always cover the cord with a spiral plastic cover intended for telephone cords. No cat can chew through *that*.

Another cause of electric shock in cats is an inadequately protected electric appliance. This is a threat to the humans in the family too, but the hazard to the cat is greater because its curiosity may lead it to inspect the appliance more closely than its humans do. Some appliances are especially dangerous to cats. Most electric blankets, for example, are sold with the warning that no weight should be laid on the blanket, but cats love to sleep on their masters' beds. Moreover, cats like to paw at the blanket with a kind of kneading movement. If they do this to an electric blanket or a heating pad, there is great danger that they may pierce the outer covering and come in contact with a current-bearing wire.

Death from electric shock because of chewing electric cords or touching a protected electric appliance is rare in cats, but it happens. More often the cat is shocked, burned, and frightened.

If the cat appears to be unable to let go the electric contact, *don't* grab the cat. Instead, take a thick piece of dry cloth and seize the wire; then jerk the wire out of the cat's mouth. Be careful in approaching the cat as long as it is in contact with the electricity, for it is not unusual for an animal to urinate involuntarily during an electric shock, and you may be in serious trouble yourself if you are standing in a puddle of urine while handling the electric wire.

After the cat has been freed from the electric contact, administer artificial respiration and treat as for shock (see above). Telephone your veterinarian as quickly as possible. He may be needed to inject a stimulant for the heart and respiration.

BURNS

Heat, friction, electricity, or corrosive chemicals can cause burns for the cat. A cat can be scalded by steam or hot water, most commonly in kitchen accidents. Second-degree burns (blistering) are rarely found in cats, though burns of greater severity are as likely to occur in cat as in man.

Any bad burn should be treated by a veterinarian. The cat owner's concern until the vet can take charge must be the administration of first aid. Any step that is taken to help the cat in this emergency must be based on the realization that a burned cat is almost certainly suffering from shock as well. So the first problem is to keep the cat quiet, warm, and restrained.

FIRST AID AND HEALTH CARE

First aid begins with cleaning the burned area as much as possible. The hair should be trimmed away from the edges of the burn. Tannic acid should be applied; the most convenient form may be weak, cold tea. A weak solution of baking soda is an acceptable substitute. The whole burned area should be covered with white petrolatum. (Do *not* use carbolated petroleum jelly or any phenol compound.)

A "baby" aspirin tablet (1¼ grains) will help to bring the temperature down and keep the cat calm.

FRACTURES

Broken bones used to mean a death warrant for cats years ago. But veterinary surgery has progressed as dramatically as human surgery in recent decades. Even fractured spines are sometimes repaired today, although a cat that has suffered a fracture of that severity probably is better off if it is put to sleep. Most fractures, however, can be handled very well by your veterinarian.

Your principal concern must be to get the cat to the vet as promptly as possible so that he can reduce the fracture. The fractured bone should be immobilized, if possible by a splint. Any rigid, straight object —a foot of broomstick, a ruler, etc.—can be used as a splint. The broken bone should be tied to the splint above and below the fracture. Then the entire limb should be wrapped in a bandage with the splint until the cat can be rushed to the vet.

If ribs are broken, the cat should be kept lying down, with the broken ribs up, until the vet can attend it.

Cats often suffer fractured tails because they fail to whisk their tails out of the way of doors in time. A broken tail is painful and it often mends with a kink in it, but it is usually not a dangerous fracture.

Dislocation of the jaw, which is technically a fracture, is common in the cat. Often it results from the cat's being struck by a car or having a door swing shut on its face. Your vet can wire the upper and lower jaws into place and in about three weeks the cat will be as good as new. For the first few days of that period only liquid food can be fed to the cat; after that, until the three weeks are up, the cat will have to be fed soft foods.

147

As in human surgery, fractures in the long bones often are repaired with the use of metal pins.

Many times what appears to be a fracture turns out to be a sprain. Usually it's best to have a veterinarian examine the area to make sure whether a fracture or a sprain is involved. If it is a sprain, an ice bag should be applied to the swollen area and a "baby" aspirin should be given to the cat.

FOREIGN OBJECTS

Curiosity, hunger, and activity can result in all manner of trouble for cats, including foreign bodies in the mouth, the alimentary tract, the skin, and the feet. Usually the first sign of trouble is the cat's pawing at its mouth or face, coughing, drooling, licking, and gnawing at its skin or feet, trying unsuccessfully to defecate, or emitting pitiful little cries of pain.

A twig or a small bone may be caught in the mouth or throat, a round, hollow bone may have slipped over some teeth, a needle or a fishhook may be imbedded in the skin or palate, a piece of broken glass may have been driven into a paw—the possibilities are almost infinite.

At such a time, keep calm and examine the cat carefully, especially in the area in which it appears to be affected. If you can find the foreign object and remove it, do so, regardless of where or what it is. If you can't find it or can't remove it, rush the cat to a veterinarian quickly.

If both ends of a bone are stuck in the flesh, it is necessary to be extremely careful to avoid tearing the flesh while removing the bone. If the offender is a fish bone, it can be cut for easier removal; a scissors will do, but only scissors with rounded ends.

A very common foreign body that causes problems in the cat is a rubber band—not only internally, by swallowing, but externally, as a result of an unthinkingly cruel act by a child. Veterinarians often have found rubber bands wrapped tightly around the base of the tail, a foot, a leg, or even a penis. In no time at all the rubber band digs deeply into the skin. After a time, the skin may even grow over the rubber band, and the only sign of the foreign object is a white, hairless ring on the skin. If the rubber band has been in place for a long time, it may be necessary to have it removed by a vet.

Any foreign object is likely to make the cat nervous and excited, so it is wise to restrain the cat before attempting to help it.

FITS

Excitement, ear mites, poison, disease, and other factors can cause convulsions. Kittens are most prone to fits which have no permanent significance. A kitten may rush about in an apparent panic for perhaps a minute, then lie down calmly on its belly, fully conscious. Often the kitten never suffers a second fit.

There are two other types of fits that are more serious. In one, the cat remains conscious, but it becomes rigid, falls to the ground with its legs kicking, and cries out in pain. In the other, the cat cries shrilly as it rushes about as though mad, sometimes frothing at the mouth, often running into furniture or other objects in its path. Even after it falls to the ground it may thrash about as though it were still running. Frequently the cat loses consciousness.

The best policy is to leave a cat alone while it is having a fit. If it is possible to handle the cat—being careful to avoid being bitten—it's desirable to move it into a dark room. Let the convulsion run its course. Then keep the cat in the dark room, keep it quiet, and apply a cold pack to the back of the head. A quarter-grain or half-grain Phenobarbital may be helpful in calming the cat. If you don't have Phenobarbital in the house, aspirin can be used as a substitute.

Remember that the fit is a symptom of an underlying problem that only your veterinarian can diagnose. As soon as possible after the convulsion, the cat should be taken to the vet for an examination.

POISONING

Despite the fears of owners, cat poisoning is, fortunately, rare. When it does occur, it is more often accidental than malicious. Frequently what appears to be poisoning is illness. For example, a dozen stray cats will suddenly die on one city block. Poisoning is always assumed by the neighborhood, but the likelihood is that the cats were swept away by feline distemper, also known as cat plague.

When cats are poisoned, it is usually because they have eaten insects that were dying from insecticides, or gnawed on painted wood, or eaten a rodent killed by rat poison, or chewed the leaves of poisonous plants. And then there are the rare occasions when psychotic cat haters put out poisoned meat or fish for cats.

The symptoms of poisoning are similar to those of several illnesses; they include pain, vomiting, diarrhea, panting, trembling, fits, slimy mouths, coma.

The most important rule in treating poisoned cats is speed. You must work quickly to fight the poison before it can do its damage inside the cat.

An emetic is the vital first step. You must make the cat vomit forth the poison. Here are some emetics that can be used:

SALT WATER: Two tablespoons of salt to a half pint of warm water. Dosage: two or three tablespoonfuls.

HYDROGEN PEROXIDE AND WATER: Mix one part of hydrogen peroxide with one part of water. Dosage: one teaspoonful to one table-spoonful, depending on the size and age of the cat.

MUSTARD WATER: Mix a teaspoon of powdered mustard with a quarter of a glass of warm water.

Note this warning: No emetic should be administered when the cat has swallowed a corrosive acid or a caustic alkali. Vomiting those substances would only burn the mouth and throat more. Neutralizing acids or alkalis are the safest means for treating this problem.

If the cat has swallowed an acid, administer milk of magnesia or a solution of four teaspoons of baking soda to a glass of water.

If the cat has swallowed an alkali (lye, for example), administer vinegar or lemon juice.

Whether an acid or an alkali is involved, the cat should be given milk, raw egg white, or olive oil after the neutralizing agent.

When the exact poison that has been swallowed is not known, the Universal Antidote can be administered. It can be made up by your druggist. It is composed of two parts of activated charcoal, one part of light magnesium oxide, one part of kaolin, and one part of tannic acid. You should keep a supply of this dark-gray powder in your medicine cabinet against emergencies.

When it is needed, the formula is dissolved in warm water in the proportion of four heaping tablespoons of Universal Antidote to one glass of water.

A makeshift and not entirely satisfactory substitute for the Universal Antidote can be put together in a jiffy. For the charcoal, substitute charred, crumbled toast; for the tannic acid, strong tea; for the magnesium oxide, milk of magnesia. Mix them in these proportions: two parts of toast, one part of tea, one part of milk of magnesia.

If you are certain what poison the cat swallowed, tell your veterinarian on the telephone. *And then—provided that the vet approves* —administer an antidote. (It's more likely that the vet will want you to rush the cat to his office.)

These are some of the most common poisons:

ANTU: rat poison used by some exterminators. First aid: induce vomiting.

ARSENIC: insecticide. First aid: induce vomiting, then give milk of magnesia and follow it with strong tea.

CYANIDE: fumigant. Kills so quickly that nothing can be done in most cases.

MALATHION (and other pyrophosphates): agricultural sprays and insecticides. First aid: ineffective. Rush cat to vet for injection of antidote.

SODIUM FLUORACETATE (1080): rat poison. Induce vomiting, then rush cat to vet.

SQUILL: rat poison. This poison is a violent emetic, so nothing should be done to stimulate additional vomiting. First aid: keep cat warm and quiet, give it two or three tablespoons of mineral oil, followed by three tablespoons of Kaopectate.

STRYCHNINE: the most common rat poison. First aid: *in early cases* an emetic should be given and after the cat has vomited it should be fed four to ten tablespoons of strong tea; *in late cases* or during convulsions this should not be done, however—instead, the cat should be moved gently but quickly to the vet's office.

WARFARIN: a supposedly nontoxic rat poison which can endanger cats in a very large dose or in repeated doses. First aid: ineffective; rush cat to the vet.

For those cat owners who may be worried about the possibility of their cats' eating poisonous plants, these are the American plants dangerous to cats: water hemlock, cocklebur, buttercup, corn cockle, nightshade, nettle, bladder pod, rattlebush, crotalaria, jimson weed, laurel, common oleander, castor bean, locoweed, poison vetch, choke cherry, and arrow grass. It is well to avoid these plants in or around the house if you want to keep a cat.

ANAL GLANDS

Sometimes you may notice that your cat is dragging its hindquarters along the ground. Most people believe this is an indication of worm infestation, but they are wrong. This action means that the cat is suffering from an anal gland problem. Another sign of this difficulty is the cat's biting frequently at the base of its tail.

The anal glands are two small sacs located one on each side of the anus which empty into the anus. A yellowish, oily, foul-smelling musk is secreted into these sacs. The function of the anal glands, as the sacs are usually called, is still not understood. One theory has it that the sacs are intended to lubricate the rectum and thus facilitate the passage of bones, pebbles, and other things. Another theory holds that the anal glands are fundamentally vestigial musk glands like those of a skunk. As a matter of fact, a skunk's musk glands are located in the same place as a cat's (or dog's) anal glands and the secretion is similar, except for the intensity of the odor.

Whatever the function of the anal glands, they can sometimes pose a problem for the cat owner. The anal glands may become impacted or infected; an abscess may even develop. When this sort of difficulty is suspected, the cat owner should try to express the anal glands or take the cat to a veterinarian to have this done. If you want to try it yourself, well and good—but let the vet show you how to do it the first time. If you do it wrong, you'll exasperate the cat and disgust yourself, for this is an uncommonly unpleasant job. This is the way you do it: With the cat on a table, facing your left, take its tail in your left hand firmly and lift it. Holding a good-sized piece of cotton over the anus, press firmly with your fingers simultaneously on both sides of the anal opening. (The cotton is necessary because the secretion spurts out when the sacs are expressed.)

CONSTIPATION AND DIARRHEA

Constipation can be a very serious matter in the cat because of the constant accumulation of hair in the alimentary tract. If this hair and fecal matter become impacted, the consequence can be more than distressing. To avoid constipation in the cat, every third or fourth day give it mineral oil, uncarbolated petroleum jelly, or one of the preparations especially prepared for this purpose and sold in most pet shops (most cats love the latter). It is helpful, too, to give the cat some roughage in its diet—spinach, lettuce, or perhaps grass or green oat shoots grown in a pot or window box.

Diarrhea usually can be stopped with Kaopectate, followed by a dose of olive oil to soothe the inflamed digestive tract. If that doesn't work, take the cat at once to the veterinarian, for the diarrhea may be only a symptom of more serious trouble. If the diarrhea recurs, the diet may be at fault; it may be worthwhile to give the cat a different type of food.

EARS

Despite its open, erect ear, the cat has a tendency toward ear problems. These include mite infestation, infection of the outer ear, tumors and inflammatory polyps, and blood tumors. These can all become serious disorders, and even in their initial stages they can cause considerable difficulty. Ear mites, for example, are the most common cause of fits in cats.

Ear ailments require the skill of the veterinarian. Attempts at home treatment are likely to end in disaster. The most important duty for the cat owner is to learn to recognize the symptoms of ear ailments. These include the cat's shaking its head, pawing at its ear frequently, or rubbing its ear against furniture. A foul smell from the ear and a black or gray accumulation of matter inside the ear are indications of trouble. Abnormal growths sometimes can be seen. Blood tumors sometimes cause the ear to become hot and sensitive and, in certain cases, to swell.

TEETH

Decay is less common in a cat's mouth than in man's. The enamel is thicker, the salivary juices are less damaging, the shape of the teeth discourages the retention of food particles, and the diet is usually better.

Nevertheless, decay and other problems do exist. Teeth are broken. Roots become infected; abscesses sometimes occur. Tartar accumulates. Gums are pushed back and become flaccid.

A good diet will help to keep your cat's teeth in good condition. Small, hard biscuits or pellets made for cats or dogs are good for the teeth, too. Chewy kidneys, muscle meats, and other flesh that provides some resistance to the teeth and gums are all to the good.

Occasionally—say, once a year or so—a veterinarian should remove the tartar from your cat's teeth. In the intervals, it is not necessary to brush the teeth.

Bad breath, drooling, pawing at the mouth, shaking the head, or pale-colored gums are all clues to possible trouble in your cat's mouth. Only a veterinarian is competent to deal with these matters. He may remove teeth under anesthetic or administer drugs to treat infections. Often vitamins may be prescribed for gum conditions.

EYES

The eyes of many cats exude a small amount of matter from time to time. This eye fluid, which dries and cakes on the muzzle near the corner of the eye, should be gently cleared away with a facial tissue.

If any hairs around the eye have a tendency to curl into the eye, they should be trimmed away.

Serious injury to the eye requires a veterinarian's care, of course, but minor irritations can be treated by washing the sore eye with a piece of cotton which has been soaked in warm water. The ophthalmic ointment listed for your first-aid kit can then be applied.

BONES

Excepting fractures, most bone problems occur in kittens rather than adult cats. However, hip dysplasia has been found in a few cats. It should be emphasized that this condition is rare in cats, although it is not uncommon in dogs.

Hip dysplasia is a malformation of the ball and socket joint of the hip. There are all degrees of bad fit between these two bones, ranging from a minor maladjustment to complete dislocation. Often the socket is flattened, inadequately cupped to hold the ball at the end of the thigh bone.

The lameness which is the indication of this condition may appear while the cat is still a young kitten or at any age thereafter. In a mild case there is often no outward sign of trouble at all, and the cat probably never will need treatment for this problem. An Alabama veterinarian has reported discovering hip dysplasia in a family of cats after X-raying one cat because it appeared to have a pelvic fracture.

Cats suffering from hip dysplasia should never be bred, for this is a congenital disorder that is transmitted genetically as an irregular dominant characteristic.

SKIN

Skin disorders are common in cats, especially in those cats which are permitted to roam. Stray cats, when first adopted, are usually found to be suffering from some skin ailment, most often ringworm. For that reason, a newly acquired cat should be examined by a veterinarian as soon as possible.

Ringworm: Few maladies are more misnamed than this, for ringworm has nothing whatever to do with any worm; it is caused by a fungus. Although most ringworm cases look alike to the lay eye— little, round, sore, hairless patches on the skin—there are many varieties of ringworm. There are several species, grouped in two genera,

155

that afflict the cat, but the fungus most often found in the cat is a species called *Microsporum canis*. This, too, is grossly misnamed; most authorities now believe that the cat, rather than the dog, is "the major reservoir" and "the natural host" of this fungus.

Most forms of ringworm—and especially that caused by *Microsporum canis*—are extremely contagious. One cat can spread the disorder to other cats, dogs, and other domestic animals, and even to man. One stray cat was the unwitting cause of an outbreak of ringworm in my own household that affected all the cats and dogs, and my wife and me. (We kept the cat, cured all the cases of ringworm, and have received so much pleasure from the culprit that it's more than paid us, a hundred times over, for the inconvenience it caused us.)

The first sign of ringworm is the appearance of small, scabby circles on the skin on any part of the body, but most often on the ears, face, neck, and tail. The cat should be taken to a veterinarian as soon as these areas appear.

The veterinarian probably will want to examine the cat under a Wood's light, an ultraviolet lamp. Many forms of ringworm—but not all—will fluoresce in this light. So will certain other things, such as mineral oil, petrolatum, and a number of skin medications. (It is curious that ringworm in calves sometimes clears up spontaneously when the animals are turned out to pasture in the sunshine, with its ultraviolet rays, or when they are otherwise exposed to ultraviolet. Never try home treatment of cats in this manner.)

Until recently ringworm was one of the worst curses of cat life. Today, thanks to griseofulvin, an antibiotic discovered in 1939 but not applied to fungus disorders for almost two decades, ringworm is a much less severe problem to cure. In treating your cat, the veterinarian is likely to follow this course: Griseofulvin will be administered in tablet form (this will be up to you to do) for perhaps a month. Once a week the cat will be bathed (again, by you) in an antibacterial fungicide, perhaps captan, which the vet will prescribe. Because of the danger of secondary infection, a broad-spectrum antibiotic probably will be injected by hypodermic.

156

MANGE

There are two kinds of mange, both caused by parasitic mites. Sarcoptic mange, also called scabies, is the less serious form, but it is easily transmitted from cat to man. Demodectic mange, also called follicular mange or red mange, is a very dangerous skin disease, but there is some doubt that this type occurs in the cat.

No layman should attempt to diagnose or treat any mange without veterinary supervision.

SARCOPTIC MANGE: This is caused by an eight-legged, round mite that lays its eggs in tunnels that the female burrows under the skin. The larvae hatch in the tunnels and feed there. The adult mite's burrowing and the feeding of the larvae cause an intense itchiness. The cat scratches and rubs constantly. The mange usually makes its appearance first on the head. The hair begins to fall out around the affected area, and the skin becomes dry, reddish, thickened, folded, and wrinkled. Crusts develop.

To diagnose scabies, the veterinarian must take a scraping of skin from the affected area. This may hurt the cat just a little, but it will help it in the long run.

Sarcoptic mange is not difficult to cure, although the treatment may have to be continued for a while before the cat is free of both the mange and the danger of reinfection. There is one problem, however, in treating mange in the cat: there is a widespread belief among veterinarians that cats are adversely affected by phenol (carbolic acid), and many acaricides—the medicines that kill mange mites—contain phenol in some form, usually quite diluted. Your veteranarian may want to prescribe lime and sulfur baths or sulfur ointments. He will also want to administer an antibiotic by injection to guard against secondary infection.

DEMODECTIC MANGE: This is caused by a long, wormlike mite that has eight short legs in the adult phase. The mites invade the hair follicles and the sebaceous glands surrounding them. Again, the mange usually begins on the head, most often on the ears of the cat. It can spread over the entire body from there. The onset of the disease is marked by sores of varying sizes, some of them scaly, with redness, loss of hair, and slightly thickened, dry skin, others with considerable redness, blood and serum oozing out, along with pus in some cases.

Deep scrapings of skin are necessary to produce the infested follicles and glands for microscopic examination, which is essential to the diagnosis of either form of mange.

Until quite recently, demodectic mange was so difficult to cure that veterinarians almost always recommended that diseased animals be put to sleep. That is no longer necessary—if the animal's owner is prepared to do the work that will be required for a cure. The work requires patience and persistence. A veterinarian must manage treatment of this condition.

Ectoral, the brand name of an insecticide called ronnel, has been used in treating mange in dogs, and cat owners sometimes ask if it can be used in cats. The answer is yes and no. In dogs, Ectoral can be applied both internally (in the form of tablets) and externally (as a dip). In cats, however, this drug can only be applied *externally*. The choice of what drugs to use in treatment of your cat, in any event, will be entirely your veterinarian's.

This warning must be added: In both forms of mange, but especially in demodectic mange, the treatment, onerous as it may be, must be continued after the cat is apparently cured, for the mites may still survive deep in the follicles. Never stop the treatment until your vet has told you that it is no longer necessary.

ECZEMA

Any dermatitis whose nature and cause are not known is likely to be called eczema. In other words, there is, properly speaking, no such ailment as eczema—but there are many disorders that are lumped together under that name. Heredity, allergy, irritation, exposure to rays, and any number of other causes are possible. Both scaly (dry) and crusty (moist) eczemas occur in cats and cause great itchy discomfort.

Follow your veterinarian's instructions to the letter in treating eczema—and be patient with him if there seems to be little improvement over a number of treatments. It would be unfair to expect veterinary medicine to be more advanced than human medicine, and anyone who has suffered from a chronic dermatitis is aware of how little is known about human skin ailments. I know of a man whose skin disorder was not cured until he had been going to dermatologists for eleven years. Chances are, your cat's eczema will be cleared up rather quickly, all things considered, even if the vet does have to go about it by trial and error, trying first one drug and then another until he finds one that will be effective in the particular case.

FELINE DISTEMPER

This terrible disease has so many aliases that it may be worthwhile to list them all: feline infectious enteritis, panleukopenia, feline agranulocytosis, cat fever, and—the most descriptive of all—cat plague.

Like the Black Death sweeping across Europe centuries ago, feline distemper sometimes flashes through a neighborhood, leaving behind so many dying cats that it appears a poisoner has been at work. But the poisoner, in this case, is a virus that cannot be seen with the naked eye. Losses from this plague are high, especially in young cats. Between 60 and 90 percent of the diseased cats are likely to die.

Feline distemper cannot be transmitted to dogs. Nor can canine distemper infect cats.

Summer is the time of greatest danger, but the disease may occur whenever there are new susceptible cats in a neighborhood; the period of greatest susceptibility is between four and six months of age. All secretions and excretions of infected cats contain the highly contagious virus. How long this virus contaminates is questionable. If a kitten is brought into a house in which a cat has died of distemper, the new-comer should be protected by serum and vaccine.

Almost all of the internal organs are affected. No part of the body is untouched; the lymph nodes are among the first to be affected and the bone marrow is among the last. The incubation period is four to ten days, and then the cat is in grave danger.

These are the symptoms for which the cat owner must watch: fever, loss of appetite, vomiting, depression, weakness, dehydration (the cat usually won't drink water, although it may linger close to its water dish).

In treating your cat, the veterinarian may resort to blood transfusions; injection of serum, fluids, salts, and dextrose; and broad spectrum antibiotics.

To protect a cat which has not yet been exposed, a serum can be administered, but this protection, although fairly good, extends only for two weeks. A vaccine is also available, but it is not altogether dependable even for its short (two-month) period of resistance. However, some breeders report excellent results with the vaccine.

PNEUMONITIS

As highly infectious as feline distemper, pneumonitis is far less dangerous to cat life. It is a long-drawn-out disease, severe in its manifestations, but it kills in less than 30 percent of the cases if the cat is in good health generally and receives proper care. An airborne virus, sprayed into the air when the sick cat sneezes, causes the malady.

As the virus goes to work inside the cat, the eyes become inflamed and begin to water heavily. Inflammation spreads to the nasal passages and the cat's nose begins to run. Pneumonia develops. The spleen may be slightly enlarged.

The cat's owner is likely to realize that something is wrong when he sees the cat's eyes and nose running. But there will have been subtler symptoms before that: a slight rise in temperature and, in many cases, some degree of sensitivity to light, along with occasional sneezing. The most obvious symptoms—the running eyes and nose—appear six to ten days after exposure to the disease. These symptoms persist for a week or two. The loss in weight which began with the first symptoms continues for about a month.

The veterinarian's treatment probably will include injection of antibiotics and possibly an antihistamine. There is a vaccine available, but it cannot be accurately evaluated yet, and it provides protection for only six months anyway. Nevertheless, the vaccine ought to be considered if there has been an outbreak of pneumonitis in the neighborhood.

160

FELINE VIRAL RHINOTRACHEITIS

This disease bears too much of a name for a small cat to carry, so it is usually abbreviated to FVR. It was not until 1958 that the offending virus was isolated. Before that, it had probably been lumped with pneumonitis. Even today it is difficult to distinguish between the two, for the symptoms are essentially the same: high temperature, running eyes and nose, sneezing and coughing, and loss of appetite. Most cats recover in about two weeks. In laboratory observations, about one of every four cats died. A cat which has had the illness once can get it again.

TUBERCULOSIS

Tuberculosis does not occur in a feline form, but cats can acquire TB from some other mammals. The cat appears to be immune to human TB, but it can contract the kind of tuberculosis to which cows and birds fall victim. In those parts of the world where milk is usually still not pasteurized, bovine TB in cats ranges up to 12 percent of all cats autopsied. Where milk is pasteurized, bovine TB in the cat is rare. So is avian tuberculosis. Some veterinary research has suggested that Siamese cats may be slightly more susceptible to tuberculosis than other cats.

COCCIDIOSIS

Cats, like dogs, rabbits, cattle, sheep, and swine, are susceptible to coccidiosis, an intestinal disease which can be acute or chronic. It is most common among young cats. Coccidiosis, which is not usually fatal, causes diarrhea and loss of weight. It is usually treated by veterinarians with sulfamethazine.

CRYPTOCOCCOSIS

An internal fungus is responsible for cryptococcosis, a disease which can make a cat's life miserable for years if it is not detected and treated. It causes localized outbreaks in the nose, lungs, and brain of the cat. If a cat has suffered for a long time with a discharge from its eyes and nose, has difficulty breathing, coughs, tends to run a fever, or develops blindness, cryptococcosis should be suspected. The disease often ends in death, especially if it spreads to the brain, spinal cord, or lungs.

TOXOPLASMOSIS

A parasitic protozoa causes toxoplasmosis, an infection that can strike most of the internal organs of the cat's body. Infected cats run high fevers, develop pneumonia, breathe rapidly and with difficulty, sound wheezy, and refuse food and water. The death rate is very high. If the disease is diagnosed early, the cat may be saved by treatment with pyrimethamine and sulfonamides.

RABIES

Rabies is much less common in the cat than in the dog—and even in the dog it is relatively rare. In Missouri, for example, over a ten-year period there were 1,368 cases of rabies in dogs, compared with 324 in cats. In a fifteen-year period following World War II, there were only 138 cases of rabies in humans in the United States, and only five of them were traceable to cats. (Most rabies in man in this country today comes from the bites of wild animals, especially foxes and bats. But in 1961 it was established that rabies can be transmitted by air—without any biting at all—which casts a new light on this dread disease.)

There are two forms of rabies, the paralytic and the furious. In the former, the chewing muscles and the throat are paralyzed, and the animal, unable to swallow, drools profusely. It usually does not become vicious and does not try to bite. Death comes in a few hours.

The furious form is more common in cats. The cat becomes alert, nervous; its pupils are dilated. It has a tendency to swallow foreign objects. The cat may seem very playful, but it will bite even when it is being petted. In a few hours the cat becomes incredibly vicious; it will bite at any moving object, including the most beloved owner. Swallowing becomes difficult. The cat may suddenly go into convulsions.

There is no cure for rabies in man or in cat. Because of this, and because of the epizootic nature of the disease, especially among wild animals, restrictions have been raised in some places against the transportation of animals. Cats being taken into Michigan, for example, must be accompanied by a health certificate issued by a veterinarian. Hawaii has a 120-day quarantine on cats, even those which are certified as having been vaccinated. Puerto Rico requires that any cat more than eight weeks old entering that island be vaccinated and certified to be healthy. Great Britain has a six-month quarantine on cats.

Any cat which has bitten a human must be kept under observation for a period prescribed by public health agencies. If the cat which did the biting has died, a veterinarian should be asked to send its head to a state public health laboratory for examination; in most states this is required by law. If it is known that the cat was rabid, any unvaccinated cat bitten by it should be put to sleep. The reason for this drastic step is simple: the incubation period in cats ranges from less than twenty days to more than sixty days—it may even, in some cases, be several months. Therefore, an unvaccinated cat bitten by a rabid animal must be kept confined, under close observation, for six months, according to the World Health Organization. If the cat owner is willing to keep his cat strictly isolated for that period of time, it need not be put to sleep.

A cat which had been vaccinated before being bitten ought to be revaccinated and confined inside the house—or taken outside only on a leash—for thirty days after being bitten, if the vaccination occurred within the past year.

There are several kinds of vaccine available to your veterinarian. Some vaccine is derived from chemically killed virus. Live virus attenuated by development through chick embryos is the basis for other vaccines. The killed-virus vaccine confers protection for about a year; the live-virus, for about two years.

163

ANEMIA

"Cats perhaps suffer more often and more severely from anemia than any other species," Dr. C. E. DeCamp once wrote in *Veterinary Medicine*. The anemia may be caused by loss of blood (from a wound, for example), the breakdown of red blood cells (resulting from some infections), or a decrease in the production of red blood cells.

The symptoms of anemia include lethargy, weakness, lack of appetite, and occasionally vomiting. In advanced cases the cat may appear restless and its breathing may be labored.

There is also a form of the disease called feline infectious anemia which is caused by either of two parasitic microorganisms. Some cats carry the disease in a latent form. Infected cats show the usual symptoms of anemia; in the acute form, high temperatures, lack of appetite, depression, and rapid loss of weight, and in the chronic form, normal (or even subnormal) temperatures, weakness, depression, and a more gradual loss of weight.

Transfusions of whole blood or serum are used to combat anemia in the cat. Antibiotics and other drugs are usually given to fight active or possible infection.

CYSTITIS

One of the most common problems in the cat is cystitis, which means, properly speaking, an acute or chronic inflammation of the urinary bladder. It is caused by infection but is often complicated by stones —those somewhat mysterious accretions of mineral particles in the kidneys or elsewhere in the genitourinary system. It has sometimes been suggested that cystitis is especially prevalent in neutered cats, but some researchers have pointed out that this may be just an illusion, caused by the fact that most pet cats which come to the attention of veterinarians have been altered.

A female cat suffering from cystitis will urinate frequently—at least it will try to urinate. But only a few drops, if any, will appear. Nevertheless, the cat keeps trying, over and over again, until it's spending a good part of its time in the litter box. It may also forget some of its house training, too, and you may see it trying to urinate in, say, the bathtub. The cat may not take good care of its appearance and the coat will look poor. Laziness and lack of appetite are also among the symptoms. As the illness progresses, the cat may have blood in its urine.

A variety of drugs are available to the veterinarian in treating this condition in the female and in the male. But the problem is much more serious in the male because its urinary passages are smaller.

The symptoms in the male may be the same as in the female, or slightly different. The male may be depressed and weak. Vomiting may occur. The urine may be scant, and darker and thicker than usual. The cat may lick its penis in an attempt to ease the pain. It will spend a good part of its time crouching. Any pressure on its sides may make it cry out with pain.

Stones slipping into the urethral passages block them. The origin of the stones is unknown. Although the stones are composed of minerals, scientists have been unable to cause stones by feeding cats diets high in ash.

The veterinarian may be able to dissolve the stone chemically, or he may have to anesthetize the cat and remove the stone surgically. Once it has occurred, the condition is likely to recur, whether the cat is male or female. In the male, it may be necessary to bypass the urethra. This can be done by creating a new opening in front of the urethra. In some cases, the operating veterinarian may wish to substitute a plastic urethra for the natural organ (the plastic urethra being wider and less likely to become blocked). After this kind of radical surgery, the cat is still able to control its urination—with some discomfort. This procedure is so unpleasant, however, that it is generally inadvisable.

When cystitis is suspected in either a male or a female cat, no time should be lost in rushing it to the vet. Cats have died in as short a time as forty-eight hours after the onset of symptoms. Often the cat's owner is under the misapprehension that the cat is constipated; before he realizes his mistake, the cat is in great pain because of the retention of urine in its bladder.

CANCER

Cancer in almost all its forms is found in the cat. Up to 6 percent of all cats may suffer from cancer of the skin, mammary glands, and bones, and as high as 10 percent from leukemia and other cancerous conditions in blood-forming tissues. Dr. Jean Holzworth, of Angell Memorial Animal Hospital at Boston, believes that leukemia and other blood cancers are "extraordinarily prevalent in the domestic cat," but often go undiagnosed.

As in man, cancer in the cat often can be cured if it is detected in time. Unfortunately, however, a cat that is suffering from cancer often will give no outward sign of pain—that is, it will not cry or moan. But it will give other signs of trouble, such as failure to keep its coat clean, lethargy, depression, loss of appetite, and the like. Any unusual growths or lumps on or under the skin warrant a visit to the veterinarian. Wounds that do not heal and symptoms that fit into the pattern of a known disease but do not respond to the treatment for that disease also may indicate cancer.

9. SEX, MATING, AND KITTENING

> *Ye cats that at midnight spit love at each other,*
> *Who best feel the pangs of a passionate lover,*
> *I appeal to your scratches and your tattered fur,*
> *If the business of love be no more than to purr.*
>
> —THOMAS FLATMAN (1637-1688)

IN EVERY society which has known the cat, it has been the incarnation of sex. Few other animals participate with such whole-hearted enthusiasm in the process of reproducing their species. This uninhibited—to put it mildly—attitude toward sex is recognized in the vulgar use of the word *cat* to describe a house of prostitution or generally promiscuous behavior.

Sexual behavior in the cat begins before puberty, in play. Kittens as young as three months may mount each other and engage in other significant movements. In this prepuberal period, even female kittens exhibit the male pattern of behavior. The reason for this, some experts believe, is that male sex hormones appear in the cat in infancy, but female hormones are not present until puberty.

Puberty occurs in the female at an earlier age than in the male. Sexual maturity and physical maturity, in the sense of complete bodily development, do not coincide in the cat (this is true of man, too, of course). The female begins to display true sexuality about the age of six months, when she may go into her first heat. The heat cycle, also called her "season" or, more scientifically, *estrus,* is discussed in

167

another section later in this chapter. Males become sexually mature, on the average, at eleven months. These ages for puberty are highly variable. In the male, for example, puberty may occur anywhere between six and eighteen months.

NEUTERING

Neutering should not be done before eight months of age, to permit the cat to develop as normally as possible. When puberty occurs, in either female or male, most cat owners will find that they can no longer postpone a decision on this question of whether to have the cat altered or permit it to remain whole.

If the cat is not going to be used for breeding—and that means most pure-bred cats and virtually all other cats—it should be neutered. Here are some of the reasons:

THE MALE: A whole male cannot be kept in the house after puberty because it forgets its toilet training and "sprays" around the rooms, and its urine has an unendurable stench. Many novice cat owners get rid of their pets at this time, sadly, because they are unaware that castration will remedy both of these objectionable conditions.

Whole tomcats insist on roaming and they are often in fights with other cats. Their unsexed brothers, on the other hand, are happy to be stay-at-homes and usually are much less belligerent.

A neutered cat is just as good a mouser as any whole cat and its health is at least as good, if not better—those cat owners who wonder if cats should not be mated for the sake of their health can be assured that there is nothing inherently health-promoting in copulation.

THE FEMALE: Many of the same arguments apply to the female, with some additional ones. A spayed female loses the wanderlust that afflicts a whole queen. It doesn't attract tomcats who would otherwise come around the house, spraying the shrubbery (and killing it) and making the night sleepless with their caterwauling.

The neutered female is saved from the stress of kittening and its risks, small though they may be. And there are no unwanted kittens to be put to sleep. This is a major consideration, for the world is full of unwanted cats that die of cold, exposure, disease, or the attacks of hostile animals. It is a curious thing that some people, in a rather obvious example of anthropomorphism, regard the neutering of cats as immoral but are perfectly willing to let the cat produce litter after litter of kittens who must be killed.

To reassure those who fear that the neutering of animals is birth control—and feel that birth control is not in keeping with moral law—Friends of Animals, an organization which assists low-income families to pay the cost of spaying their pets, solicited an opinion from the Roman Catholic Archdiocese of New York on this matter. The Reverend Timothy J. Flynn, director of the Archdiocesan Bureau of Information, replied, "I think that you should notify your members through whatever means you have at your disposal that the Church has no objection to the spaying of animals."

For most owners of female cats, the question of spaying is resolved abruptly after several nerve-wracking nights spent listening to their pets "calling" for a mate.

The neutering of either male or female can be done at any time, even immediately before, during, or after the female's season. The veterinarian who will perform the operation may have a personal preference in this matter of timing, and you ought to consult him first.

It is easier, and less expensive, to have a male unsexed. The organs are external and accessible. The cat is anesthetized and then castrated. Most veterinarians leave the scrotal sac intact after removing the testes from within it, so that the cat still looks like a male. The cat can be taken home the same day.

The spaying of the female, on the other hand, requires an abdominal incision to permit the removal of the ovaries and related organs. It is a minor operation, but the abdominal wall has been breached, and usually the cat must be kept in the veterinarian's hospital for a few days to ensure confinement and hence proper rest while the incision heals. It follows, therefore, that the operation should be more expensive for the female. The fees for neutering either sex, however, are very reasonable.

After spaying, many cat owners fear that their pets will grow fat. There is no sound basis for this fear. It is probably predicated on the fact that chickens are unsexed to fatten them as capons, but cocks are castrated at a very early age, even before the secondary sex characteristics have been developed. If any animal is unsexed before puberty, it tends to grow fat; after puberty, that is not true. If a cat is neutered at any time after the age of eight months, it should develop normally except in its sexuality. There is no reason why a neutered cat, fed a correct diet, should be fat.

Sexual behavior usually ends in the female cat within twenty-four hours after spaying—that is, before it is ready to return home from the veterinary hospital. In the male cat, interest in sex usually will diminish rapidly and within a couple of weeks the cat has lost all appetite for amorous conquests. However, in some cases—usually cats which have engaged in copulation at some time before castration—the cat may go on trying to mount other cats for months or even years. This can be somewhat disconcerting to the cat owner, who is certain that the vet botched the job. He didn't. In such cases, the male's interest in mounting other cats is not really very strong.

THE MALE CAT

In the rest of this chapter, we will be dealing with whole cats, with cats which have not been unsexed. It is assumed that an uncastrated male is intended to be used for breeding purposes, and that it is, therefore, probably pedigreed, an above-average example of its breed, and an animal notable for its physical and mental soundness.

If the cat is a cryptorchid (i.e., both testicles are undescended) or a monorchid (one testicle has been retained within the abdomen), it should not be employed in a breeding program. Indeed, it is wellnigh a physical impossibility to breed a cryptorchid, for the heat inside the body will kill the spermatozoa, although cryptorchids have been bred on an experimental basis. A monorchid can reproduce itself, but it should not be permitted to do so because this abnormality is an inherited fault. There is a relatively high level of late cancer in cryptorchids and monorchids that have not been castrated.

A cat with any genetically transmitted abnormality ought not to be bred. These abnormalities include polydactylism (too many toes on a

170

foot), posterior reduplication (two feet at the bottom of each hind leg), bent or kinky tail, and cleft palate.

A stud cat cannot be kept in the house, so it ought to have an enclosed outside run if it does not roam freely. Such a run ought to be at least ten feet long and preferably twenty. Any tomcat so confined ought to have human companionship for a period every day. This can sometimes be combined with the cat's daily brushing.

THE FEMALE CAT

The queen, as a brood cat is called, should not be bred before her second season. This may be a bit of a problem, however, if her cycle is abnormal, and estrus abnormalities are common. Some females come into heat every three weeks. I had one that came into season every ten days. I know of another cat that never really was out of season. A veterinarian should be consulted regarding such abnormality.

No queen should be asked to bear more than two litters of kittens in a year, and it is better to restrict it to one litter. The best time for kittens to be born is in the spring, summer, or early fall.

THE HEAT CYCLE

Unlike humans—but like dogs and many other mammals—the female cat can mate only when it is in season. The male cat can mate any time. Most female cats have more than two heats each year. Some scientists believe that a normal female cat never has a heat in winter.

For those cats which are in season almost constantly if they are not bred, a progesterone derivative is available to suppress estrus. This hormonal biochemical, medroxyprogesterone, is given to the cat in tablet form. Within twenty-four hours the cat is thoroughly quieted and refuses mating. The dosage is maintained for another two to four days. After an interval of two to four months, estrus returns. The drug has no effect on future pregnancies.

The female cat has the same reproductive system as woman. The major difference is in ovulation.

The first stage of the heat cycle is called *proestrus*. The uterus and the vagina undergo changes to get ready for copulation and pregnancy. The vulva begin to swell, although the swelling is not noticeable at first. The cat becomes more affectionate than usual. It also becomes fussy and restless. Its appetite may increase.

The second stage is *estrus,* the period when mating can occur. This usually lasts about four to seven days. During this time the uterine development that began in proestrus continues. The vulvar swelling is obvious. The cat becomes extremely affectionate. It rolls on the floor and calls almost insistently for a mate. It usually loses appetite.

If the cat is not mated, a third stage, *metestrus,* occurs. In this stage the reproductive organs gradually reduce their reproductive activities and enter a period of quiescence known as *anestrus* until the next cycle begins.

Ovulation does not occur unless there has been coition.

MATING

The calling of the queen, to announce that it is in the mood to receive suitors, is quite unnecessary; tomcats clearly know several days before that their opportunity is fast approaching. Perhaps the slight vaginal discharge that occasionally occurs tips them off by an odor imperceptible to the human nose and usually unnoticed by the queen's owner because the cat cleans itself so well.

An inexperienced cat should always be mated with an experienced cat, for an unfortunate incident during its first mating—an attack by its mate, for example—can limit a cat's future usefulness in a breeding program.

When the actual mating occurs, no human help is necessary. The best procedure is to let the two cats into a room together. But humans should be standing by in the room in case of trouble. At this tense moment, either cat may turn on the other in a passion that is certainly not love.

The usual mating is quite uneventful, however. The female crouches in front of the male, treading with her paws, moaning, and arching her back toward the floor, so that her head is higher than the middle of

172

her back and her hindquarters are higher than her head. The male utters a brief cry and then approaches the female from the side and rear. Grasping the scruff of her loose neck fur in his teeth, he leaps astride her back. She lifts her tail aside as he kneads her sides with his forepaws and engages in a treading movement with his hind-paws on either side of her hindquarters. There is a series of rapid pelvic thrusts, and then the male is motionless as ejaculation occurs. Then he suddenly withdraws his penis as the female cries out in pain.

The female's cry of pain is caused by the barbs on the cat's penis. These are not felt when the penis enters the vagina, but when it is withdrawn, the barbs rake the walls of the passage. It is believed that the scraping of the vagina by the barbs is an essential part of coition in the cat, a nervous stimulus causing ovulation to begin.

Necessary though it may be, the female doesn't like it, and she is perfectly capable of whipping around to attack the male. A wise male, at this point, leaps to some place of safety—the top of a chair, say.

When the stud is out of reach, the female usually rolls on the floor wildly, and this rolling may go on for several minutes. The purpose of this is not known, if, indeed, there is a purpose. Perhaps she does it because she's ecstatic. On the other hand, maybe she just hurts.

To guard against an unsuccessful service, it is customary to arrange a second mating a day later.

After coition, the spermatozoa and the ova begin their journeys toward each other. The ova migrate from the two ovaries through the oviducts to the uterus. In the upper third of the oviduct fertilization takes place as the handful of ova are surrounded by millions of sperm cells; this is usually eighteen to twenty-seven hours after coition.

The fertilized ova do not stop in the uterus; they continue on into the two long, cylindrical chambers that open off the uterus. These are called the "horns" of the uterus. The ova attach themselves to the walls of the horns at equal distances from each other, there to grow until the time of birth.

It is a curious thing that many of the ova begin to grow in the uterine horns and then atrophy, apparently being resorbed into the bloodstream after a while. The usual litter of kittens contains four, and one research group reported that the largest litter produced under

KITTENING CHART

This shows on what date kittens may be born if the mating occurs on the date listed on the top line.

JANUARY

Mated	1	2	3	4	5	6	7	8	9	10	11	12	13	14	15	16	17	18	19	20	21	22	23	24	25	26	27	28	29	30	31
Kittens	7	8	9	10	11	12	13	14	15	16	17	18	19	20	21	22	23	24	25	26	27	28	29	30	31	1	2	3	4	5	6

MARCH ———— APRIL

FEBRUARY

Mated	1	2	3	4	5	6	7	8	9	10	11	12	13	14	15	16	17	18	19	20	21	22	23	24	25	26	27	28
Kittens	7	8	9	10	11	12	13	14	15	16	17	18	19	20	21	22	23	24	25	26	27	28	29	30	1	2	3	4

APRIL ———— MAY

MARCH

Mated	1	2	3	4	5	6	7	8	9	10	11	12	13	14	15	16	17	18	19	20	21	22	23	24	25	26	27	28	29	30	31
Kittens	5	6	7	8	9	10	11	12	13	14	15	16	17	18	19	20	21	22	23	24	25	26	27	28	29	30	31	1	2	3	4

MAY ———— JUNE

APRIL

Mated	1	2	3	4	5	6	7	8	9	10	11	12	13	14	15	16	17	18	19	20	21	22	23	24	25	26	27	28	29	30
Kittens	5	6	7	8	9	10	11	12	13	14	15	16	17	18	19	20	21	22	23	24	25	26	27	28	29	30	1	2	3	4

JUNE ———— JULY

MAY

Mated	1	2	3	4	5	6	7	8	9	10	11	12	13	14	15	16	17	18	19	20	21	22	23	24	25	26	27	28	29	30	31
Kittens	5	6	7	8	9	10	11	12	13	14	15	16	17	18	19	20	21	22	23	24	25	26	27	28	29	30	31	1	2	3	4

JULY ———— AUGUST

JUNE

Mated	1	2	3	4	5	6	7	8	9	10	11	12	13	14	15	16	17	18	19	20	21	22	23	24	25	26	27	28	29	30
Kittens	5	6	7	8	9	10	11	12	13	14	15	16	17	18	19	20	21	22	23	24	25	26	27	28	29	30	31	1	2	3

AUGUST ———— SEPTEMBER

JULY

MATED	1	2	3	4	5	6	7	8	9	10	11	12	13	14	15	16	17	18	19	20	21	22	23	24	25	26	27	28	29	30	31
KITTENS	4	5	6	7	8	9	10	11	12	13	14	15	16	17	18	19	20	21	22	23	24	25	26	27	28	29	30	1	2	3	4

SEPTEMBER · OCTOBER

AUGUST

MATED	1	2	3	4	5	6	7	8	9	10	11	12	13	14	15	16	17	18	19	20	21	22	23	24	25	26	27	28	29	30	31
KITTENS	5	6	7	8	9	10	11	12	13	14	15	16	17	18	19	20	21	22	23	24	25	26	27	28	29	30	31	1	2	3	4

OCTOBER · NOVEMBER

SEPTEMBER

MATED	1	2	3	4	5	6	7	8	9	10	11	12	13	14	15	16	17	18	19	20	21	22	23	24	25	26	27	28	29	30
KITTENS	5	6	7	8	9	10	11	12	13	14	15	16	17	18	19	20	21	22	23	24	25	26	27	28	29	30	1	2	3	4

NOVEMBER · DECEMBER

OCTOBER

MATED	1	2	3	4	5	6	7	8	9	10	11	12	13	14	15	16	17	18	19	20	21	22	23	24	25	26	27	28	29	30	31
KITTENS	5	6	7	8	9	10	11	12	13	14	15	16	17	18	19	20	21	22	23	24	25	26	27	28	29	30	31	1	2	3	4

DECEMBER · JANUARY

NOVEMBER

MATED	1	2	3	4	5	6	7	8	9	10	11	12	13	14	15	16	17	18	19	20	21	22	23	24	25	26	27	28	29	30
KITTENS	5	6	7	8	9	10	11	12	13	14	15	16	17	18	19	20	21	22	23	24	25	26	27	28	29	30	31	1	2	3

JANUARY · FEBRUARY

DECEMBER

MATED	1	2	3	4	5	6	7	8	9	10	11	12	13	14	15	16	17	18	19	20	21	22	23	24	25	26	27	28	29	30	31
KITTENS	4	5	6	7	8	9	10	11	12	13	14	15	16	17	18	19	20	21	22	23	24	25	26	27	28	1	2	3	4	5	6

FEBRUARY · MARCH

their supervision numbered eight—but a cat was opened fifteen days after coition and was found to have at least twelve fertilized ova in its horns, and this is believed to be typical.

As soon as ovulation occurs, blood seals the follicles of the ovaries in which the eggs are produced. These blood plugs mark the beginning of the *corpus luteum,* a yellow cellular mass that forms over the follicles in the ovaries. It produces a hormone which ends the heat cycle.

The cat is now pregnant, or "in kitten," as we say.

PREGNANCY

The period of gestation—the time from coition to parturition—in the cat varies from fifty-six to seventy-one days. The normal time is sixty-five days. Kittens born on or before the sixty-first day have scarcely any chance for survival.

The kittens in any litter may have more than one father, although each kitten can have only one. Because of the length of time between coition and fertilization, it is possible for two or more tomcats to deposit their sperm inside the queen. Each ovum will accept only one sperm, so a given kitten will have only one father. But, because there are spermatozoa from two or more cats in the oviduct at the time, the next ovum may be fertilized by a spermatozoon from a different cat. Thus, a Russian Blue female that escapes briefly for a romantic escapade may produce kittens in one litter that have been sired by a Siamese and by a long-hair.

True superfetation, that is, intercourse and impregnation after a previous pregnancy is already under way, also occurs in the cat, but it is an extreme rarity. In one pregnant cat which was studied postmortem, one full-term, fully developed fetus was discovered, along with five embryos. And even the embryos did not appear to be all of the same age.

Usually, however, the period of pregnancy is not a time for erotic antics; it is a time of growth, when the cat will grow increasingly quiet and careful of herself as her time nears.

About the twenty-first day the cat's nipples become slightly pinker

than usual. This is the first outward sign that the mating was success-
ful and the cat is pregnant. Before another week is out the veterinarian
will be able, by feeling the uterine horns, to confirm the fact. At the
same time, the nipples will have begun to swell and grow even more
pink.

The pregnant cat should be treated normally. Until the last week of
pregnancy, it can run and play as well as ever. In the last week, the
cat itself usually will begin to show a certain amount of caution about
jumping and other activities. A few cats lack the good sense to do
this, however, and the owner of such a cat must simply try to restrain
it from overactivity until after the kittening.

The pregnant queen should be fed a good, well-balanced diet. It is
well to add nonfat milk solids or other calcium to the diet from the
beginning, for pregnancy causes a terrible drain on the cat's calcium
reserves. In the fifth week, the cat's consumption of food will increase
gradually and additional snacks or small meals can be added; the cat
itself ought to be permitted to set the pace unless its demands get out
of hand. A vitamin-mineral supplement also will help to ensure a
healthy, vigorous litter.

Some pregnant cats suffer from constipation toward the end of their
time. White petroleum jelly which is not carbolated can be smeared
on the cat's nose; licked off, it will encourage bowel movement.

When about two-thirds of the gestation period has passed, some cats
will occasionally roll on the ground for no apparent reason. It has
been theorized that the first movement of the unborn kittens within
the body of the queen—this is called the "quickening" of the kittens
—arouses the cat to this action.

During the last two weeks of her pregnancy, the cat may often
appear restless, roaming back and forth throughout the house. She
is looking for a place to bear her young. This, then, is the time to make
a kittening box and introduce the cat to it.

An inexpensive and easy-to-make kittening box begins with a big
cardboard box begged from the grocer. It should be quite large—say,
the size of a cereal carton. A door should be cut in the front of the
box, but a sill should be left halfway up, to keep the kittens confined
when they begin crawling about. The top should be left on the box

177

so that it will be dark inside, but it can be cut on three sides, with the fourth side acting as a kind of hinge to permit lifting of the top, facilitating access to the kittens.

An even layer of newspapers an inch or two thick should be laid on the bottom of the box. The cat will want to dig at the papers with her claws as she makes a nest for kittening. As the papers are torn up, they should be replaced with fresh, even papers again. When the cat is ready to take up her residence in the box for parturition, a blanket should be laid over the newspapers to make the box warmer for the kittens. When the cat's time is due, a big towel can be laid on top of the blanket to protect it from the stains of the afterbirth and other discharged matter.

Failure to provide a kittening box that meets with the cat's approval can result in her giving birth in some place that doesn't meet with *your* approval—your own bed, for example.

KITTENING

When the big day is at hand, and the cat is in her kittening box, making a nest for her young, you'd do well to have these at hand:

• A hot-water bottle, covered with an old towel so it won't be too hot for the kittens.

• A small cardboard box, lined with another old towel, to hold the kittens and the hot-water bottle.

• A rectal thermometer, for taking the cat's temperature.

• Paper and pencil, for noting down each afterbirth as it emerges.

If you have a blunt pair of scissors, keep that on hand, too, for cutting the umbilical cord if necessary. The cord can be torn with your fingers, however, so the scissors aren't really essential.

The hair around the nipples should be cut away on all long-haired cats and on most other cats. The nipples should be rubbed gently with olive oil if the cat has had kittens previously, for tissue tends to form over the nipples after nursing ceases.

Most cats prefer to have their owners near them at kittening time. The presence of the humans is reassuring. Perhaps the cat realizes that help is at hand in case of trouble.

178

SEX, MATING, AND KITTENING

Just before the first kitten is born, the cat's temperature drops below normal, that is, below 101.5 degrees Fahrenheit. It later rises to normal. If it goes above normal, something is probably wrong and the veterinarian should be called at once.

The kittens, which had been carried high up near the chest, have now dropped down and toward the rear.

The cat begins to pant. The "water" breaks. Soon it can be seen that her flanks are moving, reflecting the labor rhythms that are pulsing along her uterus.

The length of time involved in kittening varies with the size of the litter, the age and obstetrical experience of the cat, and her muscle tone and general health. Four kittens may be born in two hours, or they may take two or three times that long. An extremely long period between kittens is a possible trouble and calls for a telephone consultation with the veterinarian.

Kittens are normally born head first. As the kitten emerges, the amniotic sac surrounding it can be seen, like a thin, transparent plastic cover. Most cats will remove the sac immediately with their teeth and tongue, but occasionally a cat fails to do this instantly. If the mother doesn't do it at once, the cat's owner must be prepared to tear the sac with his fingers and carefully wipe it away from the kitten with a towel. The kitten will suffocate if the sac isn't quickly removed.

The next problem is the umbilical cord. Normally the mother severs the cord with her teeth, separating the kitten from its placenta (afterbirth). If she doesn't do this, it must be done by the cat owner. Sterilized blunt scissors can be used, cutting the cord about an inch and a half from the kitten's abdomen. The cord should be pinched for a minute or two to cut off the loss of blood through the severed cord. If necessary, the cord can be tied near the end with sterilized string or thread. If blunt scissors are not available, the cord can be torn apart with the fingers, but extreme care must be taken not to exert any pull on the kitten's stomach, for this will cause an umbilical hernia. For safety's sake, the cord should be torn about two inches from the kitten's body, with the kitten and the cord close to it protected by the left hand against any pull.

After removing the sac and severing the cord, the cat licks the kitten all over very vigorously. Indeed, she may appear too rough in

179

your eyes, but this vigor is intentional; it helps to start the kitten breathing. If the kitten doesn't begin to breathe quickly, it may be necessary for the cat owner to take a hand. This means rubbing the kitten with a towel and, in case it is choked with mucous, holding it upside down and shaking it to let the mucous drain out. Even if the kitten does begin breathing when the mother is licking it, it is well to wipe it afterward with a towel in order to dry it still more.

Then the kitten can be set aside in the little box with the hot water bottle. Be sure that the bottle is not so hot as to burn the kitten and that the towel protects the kitten from direct contact with the bottle. Do not handle the kittens unless it is absolutely necessary, and in that event as little as possible.

If the kitten, while it is in the small box, cries, put it on one of the mother's nipples for a few moments. That will comfort the kitten and the act of nursing stimulates the cat's labor pains, encouraging the birth of the next kitten.

After the sac is removed, the cord severed, and the kitten licked clean, the mother usually will eat the afterbirth. This is somewhat disconcerting to many humans, but it is sound instinct on the part of the cat. Any afterbirth that she doesn't eat should be removed by the owner, however.

Before the afterbirth is eaten or removed, be sure to note it down on the piece of paper. When the kittening is over, you'll never be able to remember whether all the afterbirths—one for each kitten—emerged, unless you mark each one down. You must remove them all, for a retained afterbirth can cause serious infection inside the cat.

If the afterbirth doesn't emerge, it is sometimes possible to draw it out gently by drawing on the end of the umbilical cord which is not attached to the kitten's body.

During the kittening, clean, cool water should be close at hand in case the cat feels thirsty. Some cats want to drink between kittens and there is even an occasional cat that may want a little snack of fresh chopped meat or a saucer of milk.

Throughout the entire kittening, remember, above all, to keep calm. Your cat may need you, and you can't help her unless you keep a cool head. And don't forget that she will sense your mood; if you are nervous, you'll make her nervous, too.

PROBLEMS

DELAYED BIRTH: This can have a variety of causes. The veterinarian should be consulted if a kitten has not been born two hours after the onset of severe labor.

BREECH BIRTH: This means that the kitten is born hind first. It is more difficult for the cat to bring forth in this position, and she may cry out and try to move about in circles. Try to keep her calm, pet her, and support the rear half of the kitten with your hand. When she begins to push in an effort to force the kitten out, you can try—very, very gently—to remove the kitten. But don't pull it or exert strong pressure. If the kitten is stuck very long, the vet may have to remove it, but this isn't usually necessary.

OPEN EYES: Sometimes kittens are born with their eyes open. For some reason, these kittens almost always die.

FADING: Occasionally a kitten will be born, will begin to breathe, and then will fade away to death, for no apparent reason. There seems to be no way to keep these kittens alive, which may be just as well. If they lived, they might be sickly all their lives.

CAESAREAN SECTION

Sometimes a veterinarian will decide that the kittens cannot be born naturally. The operation for removal of the living kittens is called, as in the case of humans, a "Caesarean section." Most mother cats and kittens survive it with little difficulty. The decision regarding such a procedure should be left entirely to your vet.

UNSUCCESSFUL PREGNANCIES

Not all pregnancies terminate successfully in live litters. Some pregnancies end in miscarriages, some are false, and some suddenly go in reverse, disproving the old saying that there's no such thing as being a little bit pregnant.

This odd and quite rare phenomenon is resorption of the embryos. The queen is mated and in due course the embryonic kittens can be felt in the horns of the uterus. The embryos grow bigger and bigger— and then, for no known reason, they begin to grow smaller and smaller and finally disappear altogether. Cats in which this process of pregnancy-in-reverse is taking place have been put to sleep and then autopsied, and it has been found that the embryos had become soft, spongy or gelatinous masses; it was clear that the embryos were being broken down into simpler life forms and resorbed into the bloodstream.

This condition, which is scarcely ever seen, is more likely to occur in old cats than in young queens. It is possible that the aging process in the reproductive system may be responsible for resorption of the embryos.

Miscarriages can occur spontaneously—that is, without apparent cause—or as a result of disease or mishap. Sometimes a cat will fail to observe due caution with regard to jumping while heavy with kittens, and may fall and injure herself, resulting in abortion. A cat which has miscarried should always be taken to a veterinarian for examination.

It isn't always easy to tell immediately that a cat has miscarried, for many queens will eat the expelled embryos. This usually upsets the cat's owner, but it is a perfectly natural reaction. Usually, however, there will be some bloodstains, even if the embryos have disappeared.

False pregnancy in animals is a rather startling concept to most people, but it does occur, and frequently, at that. It differs from species to species, however. In the dog, for example, false pregnancy may follow any heat, even without mating. In the cat, on the other hand, false pregnancy occurs after coition. The intercourse has been unsuccessful, of course, but the cat's owner can't tell, for the cat shows every sign of pregnancy. The nipples become flushed and enlarged, the flanks are distended, and the cat puts on a great act of motherhood in bloom. A veterinarian cannot feel embryos in the horns of the uterus, but many cat owners neglect to take their cats to the vet for examination, so this revealing examination is lost to them.

SEX, MATING, AND KITTENING

The burlesque comes to an end usually about the end of the seventh week after coition. The nipples lose their redness and the swelling subsides, and the flanks return to normal. There may be a slight vaginal discharge and the cat may even—in very rare cases—expel a sac which is empty except for the amniotic fluid. The cat will break the sac and eat it, just as she would have done if there had been a kitten inside it.

It is all part of the fascinating miracle of life reproduced, which must fill with awe and wonder anyone who watches the process of kittening in the cat.

10. THE OLD CAT

Nothing's more playful than a young cat, nor more grave than an old one.

—THOMAS FULLER (1608-1661)

With good care and good luck, a cat can live quite a long time—more than twice as long as a dog. These later years can be years of health and happiness for the cat if a few simple rules are followed.

Overriding every other need of the cat at any age, but especially in the twilight years, is the cat's hunger for affection. The cat may make its presence less forcefully felt because of its more extended sleep and less energetic play, but it wants attention more than ever. It should be treated with gentleness, tenderness, and the dignity befitting its years.

These later years are not the time to introduce a second cat into the household. If there is more than one cat in your home already, that's splendid. But don't light the fires of jealousy in your old friend at this late age by bringing a young cat into its private preserves. The time to get a second cat is when your first cat is still fairly young.

Like an old man or woman dozing before a television set, the old cat sleeps a great deal of the time, even longer than it did as a young cat, and all cats, as every cat owner knows, sleep a great deal of the time. The old cat needs its rest to counteract the erosive effects of time on its body.

Although the need for rest may be obvious, the need for play may be less apparent. Nevertheless, it is a very real and important need. As long as the cat lives, it will want to play, need to play. For play is exercise, the hunt, the world of imagination all rolled up in one. A rolling ball will ever be a fleeing mouse. A dangling string will always be a treacherous viper. A cat no longer interested in playing is a cat that is losing interest in living. It is the task of the cat's owner to maintain that interest in play by taking the time every day to participate in the cat's games. And there's no better way of demonstrating your affection for your old friend.

DIET

A sound, well-balanced diet in the cat's earlier years is the best way to ensure good health and vigor in its later days. This kind of diet, described previously in this book, will provide the vitamins, minerals, proteins, fats, and carbohydrates that will prevent or delay the crippling degeneration of tissues in old age.

The later years may call for some changes in the diet. The old cat certainly ought to be given a vitamin-mineral supplement, possibly one of the daily multiple vitamin and mineral tablets sold for humans. B-complex vitamins are especially important in maintaining healthy mouths.

At no age should a cat be permitted to choose its own diet, and this is most emphatically true of the old cat. On the other hand, it may be necessary to ask the cat to accept rather strange diets to meet special health needs. For example, cats with chronic kidney disease, not uncommon in older cats, may have to eat low-protein diets like spaghetti with meat and tomato sauce, macaroni and cheese, or tuna-fish and noodle casserole.

Water is as important to the cat in old age as in youth. It should be clean, fresh, and cool, and available to the cat at all times.

HEALTH PROBLEMS

In all animals, old age is a time of gradual deterioration of tissues. The degenerative effects of aging cannot be altogether prevented, but they can be slowed, arrested, or alleviated.

The eyes, the ears, and the mouth should be watched with special care in the older cat. A veterinarian should examine the animal not less than once a year, and preferably twice. The tartar on teeth must be scaled off. Loose or decayed teeth must be extracted.

Eczema is one of the common problems of older cats. Usually this is not a fungus skin disturbance but an allergic disorder. Foods, seasonal factors, and even personal habits, such as sleeping on a TV set or under a radiator, may be the root of the trouble. In most cases the veterinarian can give considerable relief with chemical skin baths and injections of cortisone.

Constipation is another frequent complaint of the old cat. The usual remedies for this problem—mineral oil, Vaseline on a paw, or Petromalt, which is especially prepared for cats (see p. 153)—will *ordinarily* stimulate a sluggish colon. Occasionally a cat will do well with a bulk-producing remedy for constipation in humans, such as Metamucil or Mucilose. Brewer's yeast in tablet or powder form is advisable. For really stubborn cases, an infant suppository will work wonders; it can be employed two or three times a week.

In extreme cases of chronic impaction causing constipation, surgery may be recommended as a last resort. A strip of intestinal muscle is removed and the tube of the dilated intestine is decreased. This rare procedure often ends the constipation problem permanently.

When diarrhea occurs in the old cat, it may be traceable to one of the familiar causes discussed previously (see Chap. 8) or it may be a symptom of chronic pancreatic disease, which sometimes causes loss of weight in old cats even when they continue to eat well. The cat defecates more often and the stools are frequently light tan or grayish and sometimes contain undigested food particles. The veterinarian can counteract this condition with tablets containing pancreatic enzymes.

Chronic pancreatitis is only one of a host of chronic diseases which may afflict old cats, for in felines as in humans the process of aging renders the body vulnerable to prolonged illness. Chronic kidney disease is not uncommon, for example. In the early stages there is a gradual loss of weight and of appetite, and later the cat vomits, is very thirsty, and urinates a great deal. Little can be done for this condition, except for changing the diet to lower the intake of protein.

Diabetes mellitus, a metabolic disease that may result from over-activity of the adrenal or pituitary glands or a pancreatic infection, is most common in very fat, old males. (It has been said that males of this description that have been castrated are more susceptible, but this may merely reflect the greater numbers of castrated males in veterinary practice. Relatively few whole males come under the care of a vet.) A diabetic cat is well-nigh insatiably hungry but loses weight. It drinks a great deal of water and urinates very often. It has a wide-eyed expression. A cat with this condition can be maintained on insulin under a veterinarian's direction, unless the disease is complicated by involvement of the pancreas or the kidneys.

Teetotalers though they may be, cats can get cirrhosis of the liver and other chronic liver ailments. The disease is difficult to diagnose because the symptoms are those of many other feline afflictions: finicky appetite, vomiting, diarrhea, loss of weight, constipation, thirst, anemia, and so on. Dr. Jean Holzworth of Angell Memorial Hospital at Boston, a confirmed cat lover as well as a specialist in feline disorders, says regretfully that "by the time liver impairment can be recognized it is usually beyond treatment." So don't expect a miracle from your veterinarian.

Blood disorders of various kinds, including anemia and an abnormally low white-cell count, are not unusual in old cats. Sometimes leukemia is involved, but often a nonmalignant condition can be discovered as the source of the trouble.

Malignant tumors are all too common in old cats, and they may be located in any part of the body. It is unusual to discover genital tumors, however, and cats rarely suffer from lung cancer. Surgery can permanently and happily eliminate many cancerous growths in the cat, and many experts suggest surgery even in cats over twenty years old, provided they are in good general condition.

If a cat does not have a heart ailment and its general condition is good, surgery can be performed at quite an advanced age. In the professional journal *Small Animal Clinician* Dr. E. F. Thomas, of Sarasota, Florida, reported on a twenty-two-year-old Siamese female which was subjected to surgery. A tumor on a mammary gland and a cyst in the chest were removed. Less than three hours after the operation the cat was on its way home. The sutures were removed a week later and the cat was in top shape.

DEATH

The end of a dear friend can never be anything but a time of sorrow, and none of us likes to look ahead to that day. But endless processes of life and death cannot be denied, and it is better for death to find us prepared than for us to close our eyes and ears and minds to the inevitable fate that awaits us all. Our cats are mortal, and one day mortality must be their lot.

With many cats the terrible day finally comes when a cat's owner must decide whether his pet is to be put to sleep. This is a decision that can be made by none but the cat owner himself. Occasionally that unhappy person will argue to himself that the cat doesn't really appear to be in pain, so there's no reason to destroy it. But the uncomplaining cat may be in silent agony from the depredations of an internal cancer; animals are stoic about chronic pain. A cat owner who keeps his animal alive because he "just can't bear to part with it" is guilty, although he refuses to face the fact, of as much cruelty to his animal as any sadist might inflict. Such a person is selfishly putting his own welfare above the cat's. He wants the cat with him—he fears the pain of separation—and so he permits his cat to suffer. For all too many of us, the last kindness we can offer to our pets is the gift of painless, merciful death, even though it leaves an aching void in our own hearts. It takes a kind of courage to make this hated decision, but it is courage that each of us must summon. It is our responsibility to the cats we love, the cats that have gladdened our lives.

Having once decided to put the cat out of its pain, the owner should put the matter in the hands of his veterinarian. It is best to have the vet come to the house to do it, but vets are so busy these days that such a visit may be out of the question. In that case, take the cat to the vet. *But do not leave the cat there!* There are two reasons for this injunction:

If you remain with your cat while it is being put to sleep, it will be less frightened. And surely the last act of love is to make the passing of your cat as free of terror as possible.

It has happened—rarely, thank God!—that an unethical veterinarian here or there has been given a cat to be put to sleep and instead, secretly and without any authorization from the owner, has kept the cat alive and used it for experimental purposes. As rare as this sort of thing is, it has happened. A sure way to prevent its happening to your pet is to be present when it is euthanized.

Many cat owners fear that the sight of the cat in its death throes will be more than they can bear. But if you are present when your cat is put to sleep, you'll find that there are *no* death throes.

It is a death as peaceful and merciful as anyone could wish. Indeed, you may think it a pity that such a death will be impossible for you when your time comes.

The cat is held in its owner's arms. A hypodermic needle is slipped into the vein so skillfully that the cat is usually unaware of it. The fatal dose—an overdose of a sedative or anesthetic—is injected. The cat closes its eyes and falls asleep, as quietly as it would in your lap before the fireplace on a cold winter night. Its sleep is deeper and deeper and then, so subtly that you will not notice it at first, the chest will stop moving as breathing ends. It is all over, a very few minutes after you arrived.

POST-MORTEM EXAMINATION

Occasionally a veterinarian will ask a client to authorize an autopsy of a cat. A few owners find the thought of such an examination distressing. There is no reason for this attitude. The cat is dead in the flesh; it lives only in the minds and hearts of those who loved it. It cannot suffer pain or indignity now. It has peace at last. All that remains is a fleshly shell that no longer even looks like the cat its owner knew so well.

By permitting a post-mortem examination, which can determine the cause of death and any other factors that may have been involved, the cat's owner is giving other cats a better chance at life and health. From the examination of dead animals come advances in the treatment of living animals. Your cat, itself, lived a healthier life because other cats were examined post-mortem. It is now your duty to repay that obligation, if your veterinarian so requests, by permitting an examination of your own cat.

AFTER DEATH

Occasionally, especially in the suburbs or the country, a cat will be simply buried near the house after death. This is unwise, unless the grave is quite deep and rocks are piled on it, for wild animals may dig up the body or workmen, building an improvement in future years, may unearth the skeleton.

The better course is to handle this matter through your veterinarian. Three avenues are open to the cat owner:

The body can be left with the vet for disposal. This is routine.

Through the vet, arrangements can be made to have the body cremated. The ashes can then be scattered over the cat's favorite outdoor places or buried. Crematoria charge very little for their services.

A plot can be purchased in a pet cemetery in many parts of the country. Usually your vet will be familiar with the pet cemeteries, if any, in your vicinity. In the New York City metropolitan area, for example, there are at least two such cemeteries, one, operated by Bide-A-Wee, in Wantagh, Long Island, the other the Hartsdale Canine Cemetery (which also accepts cats, despite its name), in Westchester County. These cemeteries have headstones and monuments and for an annual fee flowers are planted on a grave every year. Cats, dogs, trained bears, goats, pet birds, even turtles are buried in these cemeteries. The sentiments on the monuments reflect the anguish and loss we all feel when a beloved and faithful friend has gone.

11. THE EXOTIC CATS

Tiger, tiger, burning bright
In the forests of the night,
What immortal hand or eye
Could frame thy fearful symmetry?

—WILLIAM BLAKE (1757-1827)

ALTHOUGH jaguarundis, pumas, bobcats, and cheetahs occasionally are kept as pets in this country, the most common jungle cats found in our cities are the ocelot and the margay. In the strictest sense, these are not wildcats, for the dictionary defines the wildcat as any *undomesticated* species of cat, and these cats, which are kept as pets, obviously have been domesticated. This is an important distinction, for some cities have ordinances against the keeping of wild animals. A good lawyer, however, can usually defend your right to keep an ocelot or a margay.

The ocelot is the most common jungle cat in the Americas, and its range actually includes part of the United States; like the margay and the jaguarundi, it is sometimes found in the southwestern border states. It has been mistaken for a small leopard, which probably explains its scientific appellation, *Felis pardalis*. The ground color of its beautiful coat is a pearly light buff. There are horizontal black stripes on its face, head, and neck. On the legs and tail are black spots. The body of the cat is covered with black rings and dots. The tail is nearly half the length of the body.

There may be more than one variety of ocelot, for the numerous specimens in captivity, as pets or in zoos, show a wide range of differences, especially in size. Most ocelots weigh about forty pounds, but it's not unusual for this cat to go over sixty pounds.

The margay looks like a small ocelot with a long tail. Its markings are so similar to the ocelot's that it is well-nigh impossible to distinguish between kittens of the two species. But the margay grows to weigh only about ten pounds, roughly the size of a domestic cat. Its tail, however—a long, thick, expressive appendage—is outsized, being perhaps 75 percent as long as the body.

Among margays, too, there may be several varieties—or there may be several similar species that include the margay. It is known that there are a number of small South American jungle cats that differ only slightly from each other. One of them is even smaller than the margay usually kept as a pet in the United States.

The ocelot and the margay are both nocturnal, arboreal, and carnivorous. They are extremely intelligent and fearless fighters. One ocelot was found with a seven-foot boa constrictor that it had killed and partly eaten.

Most of the ocelots and margays offered for sale in the United States are jungle-born, although a few are bred here by fanciers. These animals are best purchased as pets while they are kittens, the younger the better, but it must be remembered that they were brought forth under wild conditions and their earliest days were spent in the jungle. As a result of the hardships they have endured before they reach this country, they are peculiarly vulnerable to disease and stress.

These cats make excellent pets—but not for everyone. If you do not have the proper temperament to handle a jungle cat, which is not the same thing at all as handling a domestic cat, you'd better think twice about acquiring an ocelot or a margay. Meg Merrill, a New Yorker whose margay, Monte, has been featured in national magazines, says, "You must have the patience of Job, the forgiving heart of a saint, the energy of a bolt of lightning, and a deep love of felines (it also helps if you are fleet of foot)."

KITTENS

Ocelots and margays ought to be acquired as kittens. The kittens should have been captured before they were four months old. Most pet shops can order an ocelot or a margay—they cost about as much as a show dog—and it's best to be ready to pick up the animal as soon as it arrives in this country.

Most kittens have received rough treatment from the trappers who captured them. They have known treatment that is far from maternal in animal compounds in their native land and, possibly, later in pet shops in this country. En route there have been many changes in diet, different handlers, and indifference to their needs. These babies are likely to be easily frightened. They must be treated with extreme kindness and understanding and patience.

Occasionally a want ad offering an ocelot or a margay for sale will appear in a newspaper. Usually this is a cat that has not proved satisfactory to its first owner. By the time the ad appears, the cat is usually close to a year old, and its lifelong habits have been set. There is very little prospect of changing it for the better. For that reason, it is usually not advisable to buy a jungle cat under those circumstances.

Treated with compassion and love, however, the usual jungle cat will grow up to be a loving and lovable pet. Despite the gloomy writings of some "experts," people who invariably lack personal experience with these animals, an ocelot or a margay, properly raised, will *not* revert to the wild when it matures. It will simply become more treasured than before.

Some people think that a wild animal must have more stamina than a domesticated creature. These are the people who also believe that an alley cat must be hardier than a pedigreed cat, or a mongrel dog sturdier than a pure-bred. This misconception comes from an oversimplification of the perfectly sound theory of the survival of the fittest. While the most fit among a wild species may survive in the majority of cases, they are not necessarily more fit—or even as fit—as animals which have been raised in civilization. The wild animal's diet often is not as good. It may be infested with parasites which would have been eliminated from a domestic animal. It lacks the protection of vaccines, antibiotics, and all the other medical advances of civilization.

In buying a kitten, one should always find out from the seller whether the cat has received any shots and, if so, for what disease (enteritis, probably). Were the shots serum or vaccine? When were the shots given? Remember that jungle cats have an unusually high susceptibility to the diseases of domestic cats.

An explicit agreement should be made with the seller that approval by the buyer's veterinarian is a condition of the sale. The veterinarian should be asked to examine the cat for general health, ringworm, external parasites, worms, and physiological defects.

Most kittens reach their buyers at about the age of two months. Many of them are suffering from malnutrition and sometimes this has caused, or is about to cause, rickets. The cat needs vitamin-mineral supplements that will provide a high-calcium intake. Ground lean beef, with just a bit of fat in it, makes a good diet to begin with. Then, perhaps a week later, diced meat can be fed, and the size of the chunks can be gradually increased as the cat grows bigger. Raw meat is best for the cat, including both muscle and organ meat. Pork should not be fed to the cat. Liver, kidneys, and canned foods usually won't work out because they cause diarrhea; so does milk. Sometimes a jungle cat will accept boneless fish. Celery or lettuce leaves may interest some cats. (They may go after your house plants, too.)

The feeding schedule is roughly the same as that given elsewhere in this book for domestic cats.

At about five months, teething begins. The baby teeth give way to the permanent teeth. Sometimes a permanent tooth will grow into place beside a baby tooth instead of displacing it, and then a veterinarian may have to remove the baby tooth.

As the kitten grows older, it may not be quite the size you expected. It may be bigger than the margay you ordered, or smaller than the ocelot you wanted. This is regrettable, but it's not really the fault of the person who sold you the cat. It is very difficult to differentiate between the two species when they are very young kittens.

Both ocelots and margays can be raised the same as domestic kittens as far as sleeping accomodations and other problems are concerned. But the jungle cat should be protected even more from any startling incident that may upset its feeling of security. The panic of a jungle cat can be so great that a fatal heart attack can occur.

THE EXOTIC CATS

TOILET TRAINING

Ocelots and margays are not house-broken as easily as domestic cats. It may take months to train a jungle cat to use a sanitary pan. Some of these cats, without any training by their owners, eventually decide to use a toilet seat instead. The method used in house-breaking a jungle cat is the same as that described for domestic cats. However, before it is toilet-trained, the jungle cat may use anything that contains, or did contain, water—including the bath tub, the sink, or large pots and pans.

Sometimes it's a good idea to have several litter boxes, one for each place that the cat seems to favor. You may end up with a litter box in every room. The box should be higher on the sides than an ordinary domestic cat's box, for the jungle cat usually urinates while standing up.

CLAWS AND TEETH

The same arguments pro and con removal of a domestic cat's front claws are relevant in the case of jungle cats. There is the difference, of course, that the claws of an ocelot or a margay are much more formidable than those of a house cat. On the other hand, a jungle cat may slip outside the house, especially if you're keeping it in the country on your vacation. Then it may need its claws for protection. But certainly there are sound arguments for removing the front claws (see p. 113.)

If the claws are to be removed, the operation ought to be performed only by a veterinarian who is experienced in dealing with these animals or one who has been in touch with such vets. For the names of vets with this experience (as for other helpful information dealing with ocelots and margays), contact Catherine Cisin, of Amagansett, Long Island, New York, who is an official of the Long Island Ocelot Club, or Mrs. Si Merrill, 2 Horatio Street, New York 14, N.Y. Mrs. Cisin is the author of a handbook entitled *Pet Ocelot,* and Mrs. Merrill has published *The Margay: An Exotic Pet.* Both booklets are very helpful.

Some owners of jungle cats have the canine teeth removed or filed down. This requires careful surgery to prevent a fractured jaw. When it is over, the shape of the cat's face will be slightly altered, but the animal will have no trouble eating. On the other hand, it is a permanent solution to the problem of the jungle cat that uses its teeth too roughly in play.

NEUTERING

Both males and females ought to be unsexed, for the same reasons as domestic cats. The surgery should be performed when the cat is ten or twelve months old.

PLAY

Jungle cats are extremely playful. They are also nocturnal animals, which means that your cat may make your nights sleepless by dashing back and forth across your bed. Some owners manage this problem by fixing the cat's bed in a cage and closing it in at night.

Nevertheless, the cat will need a great deal of play. All ordinary cat toys are fun for jungle cats. The toy should not be capable of being torn and swallowed, nor should it have any sharp objects inside it.

Jungle cats, being arboreal, love to climb. A six-foot stepladder will make such a cat ecstatic; the cat will climb up and down, nap on a top step, leap on and off the ladder.

Margays sometimes will lurk in playful ambush atop a door, then take great glee in leaping onto the shoulders of the first person who passes through the door. This can be an unnerving experience until the owner becomes accustomed to it. But it's all in fun, and there's no meanness in it.

WATER

Unlike most domestic cats, ocelots and margays often like water. A tubful of water may delight them and lead to all manner of games. Sometimes the cat will even go for a swim.

196

CATS AND CHILDREN

Given the proper, cautious introductions, a jungle cat will get along well with domestic cats. Mrs. Merrill, for example, has a margay named Monte (for Montezuma) and two long-haired cats. One of the long-hairs doesn't like Monte and made that clear at the beginning; Monte gives that cat a wide birth. But the other long-hair, a blue, is fond of Monte, and "fond" is a totally inadequate word to express the utter devotion that Monte feels for the blue. Monte and the blue sleep together, cuddled into one inextricable mass, and Monte is devotedly protective of his pal.

Children and jungle cats get along well together too, but it's generally inadvisable to bring an ocelot or a margay into a household in which there are children under ten. These cats are strong, energetic, and fast-moving, and they can barrel into a child and knock it over without intending any harm. A child should be big enough to cope with a jungle cat before it is exposed to one.

* * *

Given the proper care, an ocelot or a margay will develop into an unusual, spectacular, beautiful, and—above all—affectionate pet that could warm the heart of a statue. To see one of these cats, born in the jungle in a state of wildness, pressing itself close to the cheek of its mistress in a passion of love, is to feel a wonder at the great world of nature and the mysterious power that such an intangible thing as love can exert in its creatures.

12. A COMPANION TO MAN

It is . . . a diversion in Scotland to hang up a cat in a small cask or firkin, half filled with soot; and then a parcel of clowns on horseback try to beat out the ends of it, in order to show their dexterity in escaping before the contents fall upon them.

—THOMAS PERCY (1729-1811)

IT IS usually theorized that the cat was first domesticated in Egypt, but this may not be correct. Since we know that ocelots and margays are easily tamed, and that this is true, perhaps to a lesser extent, of bobcats, there is no logical reason to rule out the possibility that the cat also was domesticated in other parts of the world at an early age, including pre-Columbian America. It is true that the early discoverers and explorers made no mention of domesticated cats in the New World. But there is some evidence that indicates that the cat could have been a part of Amerindian life. For example, Frederick J. Dockstader, director of the Museum of the American Indian, has reproduced in his *Indian Art in America* a cat effigy carved by the key dwellers of Florida in the period from A.D. 1000 to 1600. This carving does not look like the sort of thing one would expect of a people who viewed the cat only as a predator to be feared or hunted. It is a rather anthropomorphic representation with a distinctly familiar air to it.

There are other indications that the domestication of various small cats may have occurred in many parts of the world many millennia ago. Sanskrit writings three thousand years old refer to the cat; as a domesticated beast, it could have been carried from Egypt to India by then, but that seems highly unlikely, especially because the Egyptians, until nearly the Christian era, did their best to prevent the exportation of cats. Ida M. Mellen, one of the most reliable American students of cat lore, has reported evidence that the Lake Dwellers of Switzerland kept tame cats about 2000 B.C. And Chinese tradition tells how Confucius watched his cat catch a mouse about 500 B.C.

That the cat was domesticated in ancient Egypt we know beyond any doubt. The process of domestication undoubtedly was a long-drawn-out affair. It seems safe to assume that it began with the finding of a litter of kittens whose dam had been slain. These would, of course, grow up as tame cats. Their progeny, in turn, would be tame. In time, the cat might become the totem of the tribe, a representation of deity in the tribal animism, especially as its usefulness in keeping down vermin became apparent. Throughout the Nile Valley the cat spread, preceded by its fame, entrusted with the guarding of granaries and homes against rodent pests.

Feline creatures which could be domestic cats—we can't be sure; they might be lions—appear on a stylized carving from Abydos which goes back to the First Dynasty in Egypt, at least five thousand years ago. By the second millennium before Jesus, the cat was a well established domestic animal in Egypt. In *The Book of the Dead,* a collection of hymns and religious texts, there is a vignette of the cat, symbolizing the sun, decapitating a serpent that represents darkness. The same collection bears other references to the cat, including the statement that "the male cat is Ra himself, and he is called 'Mau' by reason for the speech of the god Sa, who said concerning him: 'He is like unto that which he hath made'; thus his name became 'Mau.'" This is possibly the first pun in history: the Egyptian word for "cat" was *mau* and *mau* was also the word for "like." (The naming of the cat has always fascinated felinophiles, as T. S. Eliot shows in his light-hearted poem, "The Naming of Cats" in his book, *Old Possum's Book of Practical Cats.*)

The cat was deified by the Egyptians. The cat goddess was Bast (alternatives of this name were Pasht, Ubastet, and Bubastis), one of the major figures in the Egyptian pantheon. She was the goddess of moonlight, linked with the great sun god Ra, who was himself often referred to as The Great Cat. The connection between the Egyptians' night-loving pet and moonlight will be obvious to anyone who has heard a back fence conversation between a couple of cats at midnight. And everyone who has ever owned a cat will understand why Bast was also the goddess of fertility. Other aspects of this deity involved wisdom, with which the species is well endowed, and hunting, an activity for which it is admirably equipped.

An important city, Bubastis, one of the six major cities of Lower Egypt, was named for the goddess and dedicated to her worship. It is now represented by high mounds designated on modern maps as Tel Basta. It was east of the Nile Delta, not far from one branch of the great river. Bubastis appears in the Bible under the name Pi-beseth; the prophet Ezekiel (XXX: 13, 17) says, "Thus saith the Lord God, I will also destroy the idols, and I will cause their images to cease out of Noph. . . . The young men of Aven and of Pi-beseth shall fall by the sword: and these cities shall go into captivity."

The worship of Bast was not restricted to Bubastis. There were temples to the goddess elsewhere, including a famous edifice at Thebes in Upper Egypt.

The Greek observer Herodotus was interested in the Egyptian reverence for the cat. "When a man has killed one of the sacred animals, if he did it with malice aforethought," he wrote, "he is punished with death; if unwittingly, he has to pay such a fine as the priests choose to impose." When a cat died, a wise Egyptian tried to be some place else so that he couldn't be accused of its murder.

"The number of domestic animals in Egypt is very great," Herodotus recorded, "and would be still greater were it not for what befalls the cats. As the females, when they have kittened, no longer seek the company of the males, these last, to obtain once more their companionship, practice a curious artifice. They seize the kittens, carry them off, and kill them, but do not eat them afterwards. Upon this the females, being deprived of their young, and longing to supply their place, seek the males once more, since they are particularly fond of their offspring.

"On every occasion of a fire in Egypt the strangest prodigy occurs with the cats. The inhabitants allow the fire to rage as it pleases, while they stand about at intervals and watch these animals, which, slipping by the men or else leaping over them, rush headlong into the flames. When this happens, the Egyptians are in deep affliction.

"If a cat dies in a private house by a natural death, all the inmates of the house shave their eyebrows. . . . The cats on their decease are taken to the city of Bubastis, where they are embalmed, after which they are buried in certain sacred repositories."

The English scholar W. M. Conway has discussed this matter of mummification, which was carried out with the rich and with cats, but not with poor humans in Egypt. "A rich man's cat was elaborately mummied, wound 'round and 'round with stuff and cunningly plaited with linen ribbons dyed two different colors," according to Conway. "His head was encased in a rough kind of papier-mâché, and that was covered with linen and painted, even gilt sometimes, the ears always carefully pricked up. The mummy might be enclosed in a bronze box with a bronze . . . statue of the cat seated on the top. Even finer burial might await a particularly grand cat. . . . A poor man's cat was rolled up in a simple lump, but the rolling was carefully and respectfully done."

It is painful to record that in the latter part of the nineteenth century vast numbers of the mummified cats were dug up at Tel Basta and pulverized and spread on the land as manure. Large quantities were also pulverized and shipped to Europe as a cheap fertilizer. No one protested until zoologists and archeologists realized, too late, that the cat cemeteries were exhausted. In 1951 there was one cat mummy in the British Museum at London and there were a few in the Metropolitan Museum in New York and in one or two other museums, and that was all.

In 1952, however, a crate which had been brought back from Egypt shortly after the turn of the century was discovered in the vaults of the British Museum. It had never been opened. Inside it were one hundred and ninety-two mummified cats, seven mongooses, three dogs, and a fox, all from Gizeh. They were believed to have lived in the period from 600 to 200 B.C.

Four of the cats were jungle cats (*Felis chaus*), but all the others appeared to be very much like the domestic cats we know, but not identical to them. Indeed, they seemed like an intermediate stage between the Kaffir cat (*Felis lybica*) and our domestic cat. The cat skulls, to mention one characteristic, were substantially larger than the skulls of today's cats.

Inevitably, despite official attempts by the ancient Egyptians to prevent the exporting of cats, the cat began to be distributed throughout the world. We know that those restless, far-roving traders, the Phoenicians, carried cats with them from Egyptian ports, and since the Phoenicians had colonies as far west as Marseilles and made voyages of trade even along the Atlantic coasts, we can assume that they spread the cat's fame widely. Whether the other lands bordering on the Mediterranean already had domesticated their own varieties of cat is something we shall probably never know. Certainly we can theorize that the Egyptian cats were bred to the native cats in those other lands, deliberately or by accident, whether the native cats were wild or domesticated.

Only in the Holy Land, sandwiched between Egypt and Phoenicia, does the cat appear to have been ignored. The Jews must have known the cat, as the quotation from Ezekiel would indicate—after all, the Jews probably made its acquaintance during their bondage in Egypt. But there is no reference to the cat in the canon of the Bible, although dogs, leopards, and other animals are frequently mentioned. In the Apocrypha there is one reference to the cat, in the Book of Baruch (VI, 22): "Upon their bodies and heads sit bats, swallows, and birds, and the cats also."

The first known appearance of the domestic cat in the British Isles followed the Roman invasion. The Romans had taken to the cat with enthusiasm. This clean, orderly, pest-hating little animal was obviously just the thing for the Romans, a people who loved cleanliness and order and hated vermin. The cat was the only animal admitted to the temples of Rome, and even the cult of the cat may have spread from Egypt to Italy. The excavations at Pompeii exposed the skeleton of a woman with the skeleton of a cat clasped in her arms. She apparently had died trying to save her frightened pet. In Britain the paw prints of cats have been found on tiles from the Roman towns of Silchester and Uriconium, and the skeleton of a cat was uncovered in the ruins of a Roman villa that was destroyed by fire at Lullingstone about A.D. 200.

The collapse of civilization into the Dark Ages also brought the period of respect for the cat to an end. The cat was still useful for keeping down rodents, but its past association with the pagan deities lingered in the minds of men. The cat began to be viewed as a part of the nether world of black magic. After all, witchcraft was called "the old religion," and there is some reason to believe that those who practiced witchcraft believed they were remaining true to the religion that Christianity had displaced. As a part of the world of witchcraft, the cat was doomed to share the fate of other witches.

The long, horrible history of man's incredible cruelty to the cat began. It has not ended yet.

The cat became the most common witch's familiar; i.e., a spirit that acted as an intimate servant. (John Van Druten recalled this in his play, *Bell, Book, and Candle,* about a twentieth century witch and her familiar, a Siamese cat named Pyewacket—the most common name for a feline witch's familiar in medieval times.) The cat was tried with its master or mistress before the ecclesiastical court on a charge of witchcraft, suffered the tortures prescribed for sorcerers, and then was burned alive.

A typical case was that of Elizabeth Francis, tried and condemned as a witch at Chelmsford, England, in 1556. She had, according to the evidence at the trial held after she had been tortured, learned the art of witchcraft from her grandmother, whose name was Eve. When Eve taught this evil worship to Elizabeth, the chronicles said, "she counselled her to renounce God and His Word and to give of her blood to Satan, as she termed it, which she delivered her in the likeness of a white spotted cat, and taught her to feed the said cat with bread and milk, and she did so; also she taught her to call it by the name of Satan and to keep it in a basket." Satan would do whatever Elizabeth required, it was said—kill a neighbor's swine, for example—and in return the cat demanded a whole chicken to eat and one drop of Elizabeth's blood. And then he'd go back to sleep in his basket. Not an unreasonable fee for such services as he performed.

The hideousness of the treatment which the poor cat often suffered is sickening. One unpleasant custom was to toss a condemned criminal into the water to drown in a closed cloth sack full of cats, which would claw him in their own terror and misery. Public celebrations were often climaxed by the burning of live cats, to add to the gaiety; when Elizabeth I was crowned Queen of England, a wicker likeness of the Pope, filled with cats, was burned, and it is recorded that the wretched animals "squalled in a most hideous manner as soon as they felt the fire." Cat-burning was especially popular on religious feast days, including the Feast of St. John, Shrove Tuesday, the first Sunday in Lent, and Easter. Instead of being burned, the cats were sometimes suspended over a fire so that they roasted alive, the theory being that the greater pain the cat—the embodiment of the Devil—endured, the greater the merit to the torturer.

To ensure good luck, cats were often sealed alive into the walls of houses, convents, and public buildings, to die of suffocation.

No torment was too vile to inflict upon the poor beast. For sport, bowmen would hang a cat tied in a leather bag to a branch of a tree as a target for their arrows. An alternative of this unspeakable sport was to swing a cat by the tail in great circles while the archers tried to hit it. The phrase, "to fight like Kilkenny cats" comes from the game of the Hessian troops who occupied rebellious Ireland in 1798; to amuse themselves, the soldiers would tie two cats together by the tails and throw them across a clothesline to fight each other.

Cats were killed for their fur, which was used to trim cloaks. They were sometimes eaten for their flesh. The cat is still used as a substitute for rabbit in stews in some rural areas of France. In China, cat and lizard were the main ingredients of a dish called "the tiger and the dragon." (It must be said that, although the cat has been used for food in the Eastern world, it has not generally been viewed there as an object of loathing, as in the West, as we shall shortly see.)

There is some evidence that nature gave the cat revenge for the wrongs inflicted upon it, in the form of the plagues that have swept across the world, decimating the human populations. Between the sixth century and the fourteenth, the bubonic plague—the Black Death—was dormant. During this period, cats were despised in Christendom, but many persons kept them as pets and as vermin-exterminators, and they were not subjected to an all-out war of extermination. And so, in the nature of cat fecundity, they proliferated.

But in the fourteenth century the witch-hunts began. And the wholesale destruction of the "evil" cats got under way. Almost immediately the plague began to rage across Europe like a forest fire, spread by the rats that the cats had hitherto kept down. In the fourteenth century alone, twenty-five million persons perished of the plague. In all, one-fourth of the population was wiped out. And the loss of life in subsequent plagues was equally great.

What part did the butchery of the cats play in this? We cannot speak with certainty. But we know that cats were killed by the thousands before the plagues began. And we know that cats kill rats. And rats spread the plague.

Lieutenant Colonel A. Buchanan, a British medical officer stationed in India at the turn of the century, had an opportunity to study this question firsthand, in an area still afflicted with plagues and epidemics. His observations made him certain that cats were a major factor. In 1908 he published his report in *The British Medical Journal* under the title, "Cats as Plague Preventers." He asserted that there was a correlation between the number of cats and the incidence of plague. Villages with large cat populations had little plague, but those with few cats were devastated. In one village, for example, there were thirty-six cats and forty houses—nearly a cat per house—and not a single case of plague. But in another village there had been thirty-eight cases of plague, twenty-one of them ending in death. The plague had struck twenty-one homes, and only one of those homes had a cat (and that one cat was a mere kitten, not old enough for ratting).

Perhaps He who marks the sparrow's fall also keeps His eye on the cat.

The Eastern world—the non-Christian peoples—never subjected the cat to the persecution that it suffered in Europe. In the Koran, the cat is not mentioned (although the dog is "unclean" in Mohammed's eyes), but Islamic tradition is friendly to the cat. There is a story which has been repeated by Moslem writers since the days of the Prophet, of how Mohammed was called away while his beloved cat was sleeping against his arm. To avoid disturbing the cat, the Prophet cut off the sleeve of his robe in order to leave.

This recalls the stories about Albert Schweitzer, the great medical missionary and a great admirer of animals. Visitors to his clinic at Lambarene have reported seeing Dr. Schweitzer writing prescriptions with his right hand while his left arm went to sleep—because Sizi, his cat, had cuddled up against that arm and was not to be disturbed.

Cats were not always objects of hatred in ancient Europe. Before the cat-hating began in earnest, a number of leaders demonstrated their appreciation of the cat's virtues. Howel the Good, a Welsh prince, for example, promulgated a code in A.D. 936 which established a fixed value for cats. The code read:

"The worth of a cat that is killed or stolen: its head to be put downwards upon a clean, even floor, with its tail lifted upwards, and thus suspended, whilst wheat is poured about it, until the tip of its tail be covered; and that is to be its worth; if the corn cannot be had, a milch sheep, with her lamb and her wool, is its value; if it be a cat which guards the king's barn.

"The worth of a common cat is four legal pence.

"Whoever shall sell a cat is to answer for her not going a caterwauling every moon; and that she devour not her kittens; and that she have ears, eyes, teeth, and nails; and be a good mouser."

In southeast Wales this code was changed slightly. In the version that was law there, "there are three animals whose tails, eyes, and lives are of the same worth: a calf; a filly for common worth; and a cat; excepting the cat that shall watch the king's barn."

In the fourteenth century the Italian painter Baroccio executed his *Madonna of the Cat,* which now hangs in London's National Gallery. Many other painters inserted cats into their artworks. The cat was intimately associated with a number of holy folk, including St. Ives and St. Gertrude, both thirteenth and fourteenth century. Petrarch loved cats, and so did Cardinal Richelieu and Dr. Samuel Johnson and thousands of others, famous and obscure.

Nevertheless, it is accurate to say that the cat remained an object of general hatred in the Western world until the last century or so. Then, in the burst of creative thinking that followed the French

Revolution and the Enlightenment, artists of all kinds—novelists like Victor Hugo, poets like Paul Verlaine, painters like James McNeill Whistler, composers like Alexander Borodin—discovered the esthetic delights in the cat, its grace, agility, beauty, charm. As well as its keen mind and humorous idiosyncrasies, of course.

This process is still taking place. The cat is becoming more chic. It is losing much of the aura of evil, although we still depict a black cat with a witch on a broom in symbolizing Halloween. It is now respectable to like cats and to keep them.

Nevertheless, ailurophobia remains with us. Dr. Peter J. Steincrohn, who conducts a syndicated health column in newspapers, printed this letter from a reader not long ago:

"My friends have just about convinced me that I have gone off my rocker and need a head-shrinker. They laugh at my fear of cats. Even my sister says I can overcome it if I try. It isn't funny. I break out into a cold sweat and turn sick in the stomach over a little cat. What can I do about it except stay away from my cat-owning friends? I really feel stupid when I act that way. I know people who are afraid of dogs, bugs, mice, snakes, etc. Yet they think I'm being silly about cats."

Cases of ailurophobia like this are cropping up in psychiatric journals with increasing frequency. A cat-hater who once would have been honored for his piety is now pitied for his neurosis.

There are others who delight in their pathological hatred of cats. In the October, 1961, issue of a magazine called *Shooting Times,* an article appeared under the byline of Bruce Allen entitled, "Common Cat—Pest or Pet?" It recommended that cats be hunted down like any other small game, pointing out that only fourteen of the fifty states protect cats from hunters. The editors claimed "an overwhelming endorsement of the article" in the letters they subsequently received. Six letters on each side of the controversy were published. The hunters who favored deliberate slaughter of cats appeared to consider these animals "evil"—"house pets of Satan," one writer called them.

Few people are mugwumps about the cat. The dog has fervent admirers and some equally ardent enemies, but there is a large number of persons who can take the dog or leave it, who simply do not feel strongly about it one way or the other.

Not so the cat. There is little neutral ground in regard to these little animals. In general, a person either loves cats with a passion or hates them with an equal fervor. Very few people are able to take a middle-of-the-road approach to the matter.

The reason for this polarity of feeling is certainly not obvious. It has long been a theory of mine, however, that the cat—although we may not realize it consciously—figures largely in our minds as a sexual symbol. Dr. Theodor Reik, the eminent psychoanalyst, has told me that he is certain that this is true, that the clue to the extreme feelings of love and hate toward the cat lies in the individual attitude toward sex and life. The cat is the freest of all domestic animals in its sexuality. It is for that reason that Bast was also a goddess of fertility. In the bleak centuries of witch-burning, the cat was often described as an incubus or a succubus, an evil spirit who had sexual intercourse with a human. There are, and always have been, many sexual beliefs associated with the cat. On March 5, 1654, for example, Jean Simpson of Rothiemay, in Scotland, went before the presbytery at Botarie. The poor girl was convinced she had "cats in her bellie" because a male cat had jumped over the table and the food while she was eating. The presbytery found that she was full with child, not with cats. Whether this was good or bad news for the unfortunate girl is not recorded.

There is reason to believe that dislike for cats is instilled by training. Some years ago a study was made among more than five thousand Kansas schoolchildren. It was found that the very small children liked cats best. The peak of cat popularity among boys was reached when the boys were between nine and ten years old; 35 percent of the boys favored cats then. Among girls, the peak age was between eight and nine, when 42 percent liked cats best of any animal.

Surely some conclusions can be drawn from this study. It seems apparent that the children began liking cats naturally. Then, as the children grew bigger, they were exposed to an increasing amount of propaganda against the cat, in the form of cat-hating statements or such superstitions as the bad luck of letting a black cat cross your path.

The study showed that cats never lost as much ground with the girls as with the boys, undoubtedly reflecting the absurd but general belief that there is something rather effeminate about the cat, even if it be a battle-scarred tom.

The world is full of false beliefs about the cat. But the worst victim of these beliefs is not the durable cat, which has survived man's persecution for two thousand years. Rather, it is the cat-hater himself, who is deprived of the pleasure, the comfort, the thrill, the stimulation, the amusement, and the sheer delight that a cat can give.

APPENDIX

ORGANIZATIONS AND PUBLICATIONS

The organized cat fancy—that is, the world of purebred cat breeding and exhibition—is too specialized for adequate treatment in a book like this, which is intended for the general cat owner. Everyone who loves cats should, however, try to get to a cat show at least once in order to enjoy the tremendous variety of cats, compare them with his own, and decide for himself whether he'd like to take part in this avocation which is so important to the cat as a pet. After all, without cat shows we almost certainly would not have breeds as such.

The best way to find out about cat shows is to read the pet column or cat column in your local newspaper. There are also three magazines which carry news and information about cat breeding and showing:

Cats Magazine
4 Smithfield Street
Pittsburgh 22, Pennsylvania
(monthly—$3.50 a year)

Pet Digest (formerly *Our Pet World*)
240 West 75th Street
New York 23, New York
(quarterly—$2 a year)

All-Pets Magazine
P.O. Box 151
Fond du Lac, Wisconsin
(monthly—$4 a year)

There are six stud-book organizations in the cat fancy in the United States (plus an additional organization in Canada). These are the organizations which sanction cat shows—in other words, which establish the rules and conditions under which the shows are held. Information about cat shows can be obtained directly from these organizations, which are always happy to welcome a newcomer into the cat fancy:

AMERICAN CAT ASSOCIATION, Inc.
Secretary-Treasurer: Mrs. Stanley Gibson
Lakeside, Berrien County, Michigan

AMERICAN CAT FANCIERS ASSOCIATION
Secretary-Treasurer: M. Porter Walley
1104 Bouldin Avenue
Austin 4, Texas

CAT FANCIERS' ASSOCIATION, Inc.
Secretary: Mrs. Myrtle Shipe
20615 Patton Court
Detroit 29, Michigan

CAT FANCIERS FEDERATION, Inc.
Secretary: Richard P. Orman
1928 Spruce Street
Philadelphia, Pennsylvania

NATIONAL CAT FANCIERS ASSOCIATION, Inc.
Secretary-Recorder: Mrs. Frances Kosierowski
8219 Rosemont Road
Detroit 28, Michigan

UNITED CAT FEDERATION, Inc.
Secretary: Mrs. Martin Sidlo
3517 South Pacific
San Pedro, California

These organizations have member clubs in various parts of the country which put on cat shows. Write to each organization and ask for information about its member clubs in your own vicinity.

Because cats, more than any other animal, are subjected to cruel

ORGANIZATIONS AND PUBLICATIONS

treatment by sadistic, callous, or thoughtless persons, many cat lovers extend financial support to humane organizations and often participate actively in the work of these groups, which are always in need of additional volunteers. It is impossible to list all the local humane organizations in this country, of course. Here we can list only the national organizations and a few New York City groups which are typical of local agencies elsewhere.

NATIONAL

The Animal Welfare Institute
22 East 17th Street
New York 3, New York

The Humane Society of the United States
1145 19th Street, N.W.
Washington 6, D.C.

The National Catholic Society for Animal Welfare
733 15th Street, N.W.
Washington 5, D.C.

NEW YORK CITY

Bide-A-Wee Home Association, Inc.
410 East 38th Street
New York, New York

Friends of Animals, Inc.
510 Madison Avenue
New York, New York

Greenwich Village Humane League
51 Eighth Avenue
New York, New York

The Humane Society of New York
313 East 58th Street
New York, New York

The Save-A-Cat League
245 West 25th Street
New York, New York

The above list excludes national organizations which are relatively ineffectual and local organizations whose policies are such as to lay them open to severe criticism by humanitarians.

Although the present writer is not in sympathy with the antivivisectionist point of view, the strong sentiments of many cat lovers on this subject make some mention of this issue unavoidable. I believe that the most effective and well operated antivivisectionist organization is the Vivisection Investigation League, 11 East 44th Street, New York 17, New York.

BOOKS

Rare, out-of-print, and hard-to-get cat books often can be purchased from the Coronet Book Shop, Box 817, Slidell, Louisiana, which specializes in cat books. Its catalog of cat books is available in answer to a letter of inquiry.

The most complete bibliography of cat books appears in *The Tiger in the House,* one of the books listed below. It is a bibliography highly recommended to anyone who wishes to delve deeply into cat lore. Van Vechten's book itself is one of the most charming works ever published on the cat, and an indispensable volume on the shelf of any cat lover.

The following is a partial list of cat books:

Aberconway, Lady Christabel (ed.), *A Dictionary of Cat Lovers,* London, 1949. Interesting vignettes and quotations.

Adamson, Joy, *Born Free,* New York, 1960. The true story of a wild lioness that grew up as a pet. *Living Free,* New York, 1961. A sequel, about the lioness and her cubs.

Blair, W. Frank, *et al., Vertebrates of the United States,* New York, 1957. A scientific survey.

Brown, Beth (ed.), *The Wonderful World of Cats,* New York, 1961. Stories, mostly for younger readers, by Lafcadio Hearn, Lewis Carroll, Rudyard Kipling, and others.

Cisin, Catherine, *Pet Ocelot,* Amagansett, N.Y., 1961. By a founder of the Long Island Ocelot Club.

Clarke, Frances E. (ed.), *Of Cats and Men,* New York, 1961. Essays and short stories about the cat by famous writers.

ORGANIZATIONS AND PUBLICATIONS

Colbert, Edwin H., *Evolution of the Vertebrates,* New York, 1955. A superb scientific survey.

Corbett, Jim, *Man-Eaters of Kumaon,* New York, 1946. An exciting and oddly compassionate firsthand account of the tigers and leopards of India by an expert.

Darlington, Philip J., Jr., *Zoogeography,* New York, 1957. An analysis of the geographical distribution of animals.

Drimmer, Frederick (ed.), *The Animal Kingdom,* New York, 1954. A three-volume survey, written for laymen, of the world's fauna.

Dukes, H. H., *The Physiology of Domestic Animals,* Ithaca, N. Y., 1955. A veterinary text.

Eddy, Frederick B., "The Panther of the Hearth," *The National Geographic Magazine,* November, 1938.

Froman, Robert, *The Nerve of Some Animals,* Philadelphia, 1961. True stories about wild animals, including pumas and jaguars, in their encounters with man.

Gay, Margaret Cooper, *How to Live with a Cat,* New York, 1953. A light-hearted handbook.

Grey, Zane, *Roping Lions in the Grand Canyon,* New York, 1924. A true account of puma hunts by the famous author of Westerns.

Groder, Morris L., *Tricks and Training for Cats,* Fond du Lac, Wisconsin, 1959.

Hagan, William Arthur, and Dorsey William Bruner, *The Infectious Diseases of Domestic Animals,* Ithaca, New York, 1957. A veterinary text.

Howey, M. Oldfield, *The Cat in the Mysteries of Religion and Magic,* New York, 1956. An invaluable study, from the ancient Egyptians to the present day.

Joy, Charles R., *The Animal World of Albert Schweitzer,* Boston, 1959.

Jude, A. C., *Cat Genetics,* Fond du Lac, Wisconsin, 1955. Indispensable to the serious breeder and exhibitor.

Krutch, Joseph Wood, *The World of Animals,* New York, 1961. A magnificent collection, subtitled: "A treasury of lore, legend, and literature by great writers and naturalists from the 5th century B.C. to the present."

Lockridge, Frances and Richard, *Cats and People,* Philadelphia, 1950. Facts and opinions about the cat by a mystery-writing couple.

Mellen, Ida M., *A Practical Cat Book,* New York, 1939. A manual of care.

———, *The Science and the Mystery of the Cat,* New York, 1949. Cat lore.

Merck Veterinary Manual (2nd ed.), Rahway, N. J., 1961. A veterinary handbook of diagnosis and treatment.

Merrill, Meg, *The Margay: An Exotic Pet*, New York, 1961. An authoritative booklet.

Morris, Mark L., *Nutrition and Diet in Small Animal Medicine*, Denver, 1960. A veterinary text.

Pond, Grace, *The Observer's Book of Cats*, London, 1959.

Repplier, Agnes (ed.), *The Cat*, New York, 1912. "Being a record of the endearments and invectives lavished by many writers upon an animal much loved and much abhorred."

Sanderson, Ivan T., *Living Mammals of the World*, New York, n.d. Contains the best survey of the entire cat family.

Scott, John Paul, *Animal Behavior*, Chicago, 1958. A report on scientific observations.

Scott, W. S. (ed.), *A Clowder of Cats*, London, 1946. An anthology of writings about the cat.

Simpson, George Gaylord, *Principles of Animal Taxonomy*, New York, 1961. An outline of zoological classifications.

Sinnott, Edmund W., *et al.*, *Principles of Genetics*, New York, 1958. A scientific text on inheritance.

Soderberg, P. M., *The Care of Your Cat*, New York, 1957. A manual by a British expert.

———, *Pedigree Cats*, London, 1957. The best text on the breeding and exhibition of purebred cats.

Stanek, V. J., *Introducing the Cat Family*, London, n.d. Contains many photographs of rare wild cats.

Van Vechten, Carl, *The Tiger in the House*, New York, 1960. The greatest book ever written on the lore of the cat.

Vesey-Fitzgerald, Brian, *Cats*, London, 1957. A superb paperback.

Worden, Alastair N., and W. Lane-Petter (eds.), *The UFAW Handbook on the Care and Management of Laboratory Animals*, London, 1959. An enormous (951-page) manual, prepared by the Universities Federation for Animal Welfare, which contains some excellent material on the cat.

Young, Stanley P., *The Bobcat of North America*, Harrisburg, Pennsylvania, and Washington, D.C., 1958. A fascinating, comprehensive work by the foremost expert on these animals.

INDEX